Chapter 1 - The fainters

Over time and with a lot of experience, it has become easy to figure out when someone is going to faint, and then counteract it. When a phlebotomist starts out, it's an entirely different story, so I do have stories of people who have fainted in the chair. We are trained during our course to handle people who have fainted, but this is nothing like the reality. Here are some stories of some unusual fainters, and what happened when they finally woke up.

The fainter who wouldn't wake up

I was in a daytime room in a medical centre for a week and was a relief, which means I went from room to room with a roster covering other phlebotomists' shifts. I remember the whole week being in this room at the time, because 3 major incidents had occurred. Two of those incidents related to work. The other incident was personal.

The first incident was on a Monday morning. A man walked into the small collection centre. The room was too small for a bed, so if I needed a bed, I had to ask the nurses in the treatment room of the medical centre if I could use one of their beds. On this day, there was no plan or request to use a bed.

I did the blood test, and everything appeared fine until right at the end when he fainted in the chair. At the time, I was less experienced with people who faint. I had only worked for the company for several months by that time so patients who fainted were a bit of a shock to me.

I then ran to find a doctor to help me. By this time, I was desperate to find anyone who could help as time was of the essence. The nurses hadn't arrived at that time, or were elsewhere while they were opening up their area. I quickly found out a doctor who was available and knocked on his door begging for help.

The doctor came straight away and got the patient on the floor. The patient then woke up as soon as his head touched the floor. It was at this time that I knew exactly what to do in relation to all other patients who faint - get them as fast as possible onto the floor.

The doctor then got his equipment out and checked the patient. He told the patient to lie on one of the beds in the treatment room until the doctor was satisfied that the patient could leave the medical centre. The patient was from then on under the doctor's care.

The next day, I went to work early and all of a sudden shortly before opening time the medical staff and I heard screaming coming from just outside the medical centre. There was a woman screaming very loudly, trying for anyone to notice her. She was right next to a car. Inside the car was a man who was unconscious. Her screams told us that her son had collapsed.

One of the receptionists said loudly there were no doctors as the medical centre hadn't opened yet. I begged her to call the ambulance. We were all in shock over the situation, and it rattled all of us until one of the doctors came walking very quickly straight to the car.

The woman was frantic and begging the doctor to save her son. I went out to try to help, but was quite useless with where anything the doctor had asked for was. All I could do was try to calm the woman down so the doctor could do her job. This doctor was amazing, and saved the son's life shortly before the ambulance came.

The third incident came on a Thursday afternoon. I was leaving the same workplace, and when I got home the police were everywhere in the apartment building that I lived at. I drove very slowly into the driveway of the apartment complex until I had reached my parking spot. A neighbour told me that, in one of the apartments, a man and his friend died by a drug overdose that could have appeared suspicious. The police asked me a number of questions at a much later time because it appeared that I was the last neighbour to have seen him alive.

Everything certainly does appear to happen in threes!

The snorer

I had been working for a while and at one stage was given a collection centre room within a medical centre for one day per week in the mornings. By this time, I had stopped being a relief. The bosses thought that I should have more stable workplaces. This is what the company usually does, after a phlebotomist has been a relief for a while.

A rather large man walked into the room. He was about double the size of me, in height and weight. The room was on the small side. I asked my usual - if he had any water to drink before the blood test. Water isn't just allowable. It can be a requirement. He hadn't had any. I asked him if he wanted some. He said no, he didn't like drinking water, so he kept refusing it. He told me he barely drank water as it was.

So I did the blood test. It was all going exactly as plan, until all of a sudden he put his head back and started snoring very loudly. There was nothing to say this was going to happen. One moment he was talking to me, and the next he was telling the whole building how he slept, loudly.

So I slowly pulled him off the chair and got him onto the floor. He ended up hitting his back on the foot stool on the way down. As soon as he was on the floor, he woke up and tried to stand up. I told him to lie back down as he had fainted and accept the water he kept refusing before the needle had gone into his arm.

A determined woman

Many patients come into the collection room with just a couple of tests from the doctor. These tests are very typical and are requested numerous times by doctors. Sometimes, they are for iron due to infusions, to see whether the infusion worked.

A woman came into the room with a form for those tests, so not a lot of sample would have been required. The collection room was on the large side, with a bed and extra room for a few people to join the party.

So I asked the woman if she has ever fainted. She said yes, with every single blood test that she had ever had. I asked her to lie on the bed. She said no. I then begged her to lie on the bed. She told me that because there's so few tests, she's determined not to faint and she *wanted* to sit in the chair. I then told her that I'd take the most minimum possible, but I had preferred she lie down for it.

I did the blood test, and as I promised I took the minimum amount required for the lab to successfully test for the results to the patient's doctor. I kept asking her if she felt as if she was going to faint. She said no, she felt fine. I finished, and then asked her how she was feeling and if she was going to faint. She then said yes, and fainted in the chair.

She had a friend with her for the whole time. This friend stood there in shock, not knowing what to do or how to help. She was rooted to the spot.

I was now very loudly telling the patient 'wake up, wake up' in a quest to see if she would actually be able to knock herself out of her unconsciousness. I then asked her friend to help me get her on the floor. Her friend didn't move.

It quickly became imperative that I got the patient onto the floor as urgently as possible. I grabbed one leg, and demanded that the friend help me pull her off the chair using the other leg. The friend finally became active, and helped me get her friend to the floor where she finally became conscious as soon as her head touched the floor.

It took a while for her to become lucid enough to explain how she felt while she was unconscious, and it was quite scary. She appeared to have been in another world at the time. As this was a few years ago now, my memory has faded on where her other world was, but things would have become dire if we weren't able to finally get her on the floor.

As I used to faint everywhere when I was younger and with prior experience learned from doctors, I knew that getting all patients to the floor would be the only option to wake the patient up. It's what also used to be done to me.

After some time had passed, I was able to advise all patients waiting outside for me that I was going to take quite a bit longer, and I asked all patients to go elsewhere if they didn't want to wait. They all left the waiting area.

I then told the patient in the room to go onto the bed. I deliberately made her look at all the incident paperwork I had to fill out, and I filled it all out slowly and meticulously, just to show her what we have to do when someone faints. She then told me that when she last fainted, nobody had filled out incident paperwork afterwards. This was highly likely because the phlebotomist was focusing on ensuring the patient was well enough to leave the room.

After this incident, the patient promised that for every single blood test she had, she would be lying down for the rest of her life.

The pregnant woman

Early on in my career, I was rostered to a small room that had a bit of a problem. In one week, not less than four people fainted. It was summer at the time, and quite hot. As I was new, I kept forgetting to put the air conditioner on, although the fan was running constantly.

This collection centre had two rooms, and the other room had a bed. I kept being told by the other phlebotomist that all these people who fainted should have waited for her in order to use the bed, but none of the patients knew they were the fainting sort until the incidents occurred.

Towards the end of this particular week, I was sure the room was cursed.
This one particular woman had all the pregnancy tests, including urine, but there was one test that stood out amongst all the others. She needed a urea breath test.

A urea breath test involves for a person not to eat or drink anything for 4 to 6 hours, minimum. It is also a 10 minute test, with a timer. As this woman was studying to be a doctor, she knew the requirements to this test, so had completed the strict fasting required for all tests.

So I started the breath test, then moved on to the blood test, which had 4 tubes, all colour coordinated. Half way through and without much indication from her, she started sliding off the chair. While sliding, her bladder relaxed onto my pants, fully soaking them in the process.

I yelled very loudly, begging for help, and another phlebotomist came to my rescue. We got her onto the floor, and she woke up. This was all during the 10 minutes for the urea breath test. By the time she became lucid a couple of minutes later, she wanted to continue with the end of the breath test, which involved blowing into a balloon. The room then became off limits to patients for at least 20 minutes after this event.

So the breath test was successfully completed, I was soaked, and the urine tests would have needed to be done later, along with the few tests I wasn't able to finish. She ended up in the other room lying on the bed, and the air conditioner was put on. As I lived near the room, I went home to change to another pair of pants, and then drove back to finish my shift. One of the other phlebotomists very helpfully cleaned the floor, to enable at least one room to be used for the patients still waiting to have their blood tests.

The woman who wouldn't let go

For this story, I had been relieving other phlebotomists for quite some time. I thoroughly enjoyed this period of my career, as it meant I moved around and enjoyed different sceneries.

There was one room within a medical centre which had just been opened up. Everything about the room was new, but there was one problem with it which became painfully obvious early on. Complaints were made from different phlebotomists about this problem, which I hope has since been rectified.

There were no blinds or curtains on the windows. The sun came shining into the room and made it extremely hot, especially during summer. People who faint generally do so more often when it's hot and when they assume the requirement is that fasting means having no water.

At the time, there was also no room for a bed. The room was slightly too small to fit much of anything other than the essentials into it, which meant that if someone needed to lie down, the phlebotomist had to ask the reception desk or nurse within the medical centre whether there was an available bed for any prospective fainters. Some people who have fainted before can forget that they do actually faint.

On this day, this lovely woman came into the collection room with the intention on getting some simple blood tests done. She sat down in the chair and I started the blood test. I got everything required for the test, and then all of a sudden I notice that the blood within the tubes had stopped. Seconds later, she fainted.

I then pulled her legs down to get her on the floor. She was at the foot step and she curled her arm around the bar at the lower area of the chair. She wouldn't let go! I did everything I could to uncurl her arm from the chair, and she held on even harder. I said loudly 'let go, let go' to very little avail. It was quite a battle!

I was finally successful, and got her onto the floor where she woke up. She became lucid, and told me she used to faint, but hadn't for so long she thought she would have been fine. She then told me she was in a dream state where she thought she was going to come to a bad end if she had let go. I made sure that she's ok, and then went to the reception desk where she was taken to a doctor to be seen about the incident.

The girl who didn't have a blood test

It was a Saturday, and I was at one of the busiest collection centres in Perth on my own. It was well known for being so busy, the complaints to the medical centre usually kept rolling in about waiting times. The medical centre staff loved me, because the complaints were less than usual and I would be trying my best to get everyone in and out as soon as possible.

I am the sort of person who forgets names, faces, and which number would come next for whoever was waiting. All I thought about was focusing on clearing the waiting room of people. It made for a humorous time, as many people in the waiting room kept laughing as I said 'number… who's next?'.

On this particular day, there had been 20 people waiting for me for 3 solid hours of a 4 hour shift. It was intense, and extreme. I had taken the numbers away at around 11:15am and there were still many people waiting in the medical centre waiting room.

The third last patient was a young girl with her mother who had been waiting around 2 hours for a blood test. From memory, on that particular day I had probably done blood tests on around 30 patients for the entire morning, so many people had walked through the door by the time this young girl sat on the bleeding chair. She was hungry and thirsty, which didn't bode well.

I got everything ready for the blood test. Her mother kept telling her it was nothing major or dramatic, and she would feel better after having the blood test done and they were on their way. Unfortunately, the build up of 2 hours waiting for a blood test was far too much for the girl, and before I had even put the needle anywhere near her, she had fainted.

Her mother and I got her onto the floor, which ensured she immediately woke up. I gave her water and whatever sugary sustenance I could find for her. I then told the mother and daughter that this particular centre was never going to be the place for them to have the daughter's blood test because the wait was far too long, even for patients who are ok with waiting. I suggested other places that had a much less wait time, and said I was not going to do her blood test on that day.

I then advised the other patients waiting that I would be taking a while, but they still wanted to wait for me to get their tests done. As they still had a number, there was nothing I could do but complete their tests after the daughter felt well enough to get up and leave with her mother. I ended up being a little late leaving the centre that day.

The brother

When I first started working, it was mandatory to complete six weeks of training and a minimum number of patients with a mentor. I had several mentors, and went to several different collection centres for my training.

During this particular episode, I was in a fairly large centre with my mentor for a week. A teenage girl walked in with her mother and brother. The room could fit all 5 people in it, with the mother and brother standing near the door. The whole family were from another country and spoke another language.

At all times, the mentor had to ask permission for me to complete the blood test, and both the mother and the teenage girl said yes. The girl had good veins and it was an easy blood test, but I was *very* inexperienced at the time. Unfortunately, I pulled the needle out too soon and a blood spill occurred, going down the chair and onto the floor.

Both the mentor and I were looking at the girl, frantically asking her if she was alright. She kept saying yes, she was fine. We started cleaning up the spill and had completed all other procedures, and it was at this time that we looked behind us.

The girl's brother had fainted! He was lying on the floor in front of the doorway. The mother was tending to her son, and my mentor got an ice pack from the freezer right next to the son to try to wake the boy up. She had to apologise to the mother as the boy was in the way of all the essential areas necessary to look after him.

It was then that the girl asked her mother if she could leave in their mother tongue. The mother became very upset with the girl and told her 'you can't leave. Your brother is blocking the doorway'.

My mentor finished first aid on the boy, and they finally left. As it was near to the end of the day, we finished our duties and left.

Chapter 2 - Swabs

Swabs can be requested by doctors for any number of reasons. Sometimes, towards the end of a pregnancy a woman would need to do some swabs to make sure everything is ok. At other times, for sexually transmitted diseases (STDs) a doctor can decide to request for swabs to be used in certain areas of the body. Another reason for a doctor to request for swabs is if a patient needs to have an MRSA test done, to check for golden staph. It's always up to the doctor which tests they believe a patient needs to do which would help the patient the most.

Generally, for chlamydia and gonorrhoea the doctor will ask for a urine test, but some doctors love to be thorough. One lovely doctor went the full hog, and requested for urine as well as swabs in every orifice imaginable. It has been a bit of a surprise to some patients to find out where and how a swab would need to be used.

Some stories of swabs can overlap with the stories I have with the LGBTQIA+ community, so I will tell those stories within that chapter instead.

The young man with African heritage

I was doing afternoon shift in a very busy centre, which had many doctors sending patients with request forms regularly. This one very young man had a confidence about him where he may have come from some kind of rap band. He walked as if he knew the dark side of life, and where he assumed he owned the world.

His doctor asked for the typical STD check, but had decided to add in a nice little surprise for the young man - a urethral swab. This is a swab that is very thin for a reason. It goes into the eye of a man's penis, where the patient had to very quickly swirl it around before taking it out and putting it into the container.

I explained what had to happen to this young man and he turned white as a ghost. All the colour drained from his face when he realised exactly what had to happen while he was in the bathroom after the blood test. His confidence within himself and of life disintegrated quickly.

I did his blood test, and then gave him the swab and explained where the bathroom was, and I showed him the box to put the swab in afterwards. A part of me thought he wasn't going to be able to bring himself to do it, but I did end up seeing the swab in the box later on. While he no longer had the confidence, he certainly had the courage.

The very professional man

I am not entirely sure why the doctor wanted the results for a urethral swab for this particular man, who had a professional career. The man had requested for an STD check, which was not a surprise in itself. The urethral swab was definitely a surprise for me, though.

This doctor may have decided to be thorough due to the man's profession. I am not entirely sure, but I had asked the man if he had done this type of test before, and he hadn't. He was closer to 50 than 20, and had no need to do this test at any time prior to then.

I explained what he had to do, and while he took a few breaths he told me he had been through worse than this and it should be no big deal for him to do it. I had told him that it was easier for women to do this kind of test as 'we have a bigger hole for the swab then men do'. He laughed at that, which probably relaxed him further. I then completed the blood test and gave him the swab to do in the bathroom. He then went to the bathroom, and did the swab with no problems whatsoever. I found the swab in the box a short while later.

The pregnant woman

Every woman who becomes pregnant has the STD checks. Typically, for chlamydia and gonorrhoea they do the urine tests, filling two jars of urine up to a required amount so both could be tested. It is not a major thing, and while there are other tests that would need to be completed, the STD check is something phlebotomists look out for.

I was at a centre that wasn't as busy, and there was a doctor there who didn't just request for the urine to be done. This doctor had also requested for throat, vaginal and anal swabs. The centre kept running out of the required swabs all the time, due to how thorough this doctor was. I couldn't get enough swabs, and this doctor kept giving the patients the wrong swabs for these tests which wouldn't give the proper results, all because they had also run out. I then had to either throw out the used wrong swabs, or replace the swabs with the right ones.

This particular patient had a bit of a problem with the anal swab. She had to go into the bathroom to do it, and was *very* reluctant. I told her I could write on the form that she hadn't wanted to do the test, but she liked the doctor so decided to do it. The patient was slightly less reluctant to do the vaginal swab.

The throat swab was much easier to complete, and something that I could do. This swab was done straight after the blood tests. The patient then became very reluctant to go into the bathroom for the other swabs and urine.

After a while, she came out of the bathroom and I by chance met her in the corridor to see the next patient. She gave me the swabs and urine, and said 'I never want to do that swab EVER again'. I told her I didn't blame her, and then said goodbye as she left the medical centre.

The very difficult throat swab

This was a while into my career so I had some experience by this time. A woman came into the collection room. The room was large enough. I had been given this room by the bosses, so wasn't moving around as a relief by this time.

A throat swab was required. I explained to the woman how her tongue must be brought down, to stick her tongue out and say 'aaahhh' and all sorts of tricks to try to get the required sample. Nothing worked. The more I tried to get her to put her tongue down to get to the back of the throat, the more she started fighting against it.

As I was unsuccessful with the first swab, I then got another swab out. I then got the tongue depressor out, as well. I knew I was in one hell of a battle in trying to get this sample, and the more I pushed her tongue down with the depressor, the more she fought it.

I finally was able to just get the sample. It was one of the most difficult swabs I have been successful with.

The woman was extremely offended by this point. She said 'I really couldn't help myself, you know'. I told her I knew, and that this was just me trying to do my job and get the sample the doctor had requested. It had nothing to do with me, but rather what we have to do to comply with the doctor's request.

That still didn't help her, and I never saw her again. I'm hopefully guessing that she realises that all the blood tests in the world would be better than a throat swab.

The nurse

Golden staph is a major problem in hospitals, so once in a while a nurse or other health professional would get their MRSA swabs done to ensure they didn't have it. They can go to any company, but because public pathology has such a long wait, sometimes patients go to any centre. I have had quite a few patients come in for their MRSA swabs, but this one nurse stuck out in my memory.

She came in for bloods and MRSA swabs. While I was getting ready, we had a long chat about the health industry.

She then told me that getting the bloods done was not nearly as bad as getting the swabs done, as she had had it before and it was extremely uncomfortable.

I first did the throat swab, and she gagged. Then I did the nasal swab, and she started crying. As they were MRSA swabs, both needed to go *really* deep. I apologised for making her uncomfortable, and she told me not to apologise, because if she wasn't gagging and crying then I hadn't done it right.

As health professionals, we all get along because we know how difficult it is to be in the profession. We look after each other. This is just one of many stories where we know what's involved, and we accept the consequences of what needs to be done.

Chapter 3 - The cancer patients

Many patients come in with the diagnosis of cancer. For men, it's much easier to find veins, unless they have undergone breast cancer and needed lymph nodes out. Men can get breast cancer, although it's not as common as women getting breast cancer.

There are so many different types of cancer, and they are all treated in different ways. Some specialists would prefer immunotherapy, others would prefer chemotherapy, then there's surgery, or a combination of the three at various times. It really depends on the patient, the cancer, and the specialist.

For phlebotomists, we show compassion for the road cancer patients must travel. Their specimens are always treated as urgent, no matter when they have their treatment. I also usually use a butterfly needle to make the blood tests as gentle as possible.

The woman with metastatic cancer

I had been working for a while as a relief at the time of this story, so this was a centre that I visited for only a week, and it was early afternoon on a Friday.

I don't do many wrist bleeds. The reason why is because there's many risks involved, plus it causes the most pain and pain is something phlebotomists try not to do. When it comes to breast cancer patients, when one arm has had lymph nodes taken out in one area, phlebotomists can't go into that arm because it will cause blood clots and could kill the patient. We therefore go on the overused arm, for which more often than not the veins have collapsed.

For this patient, however, there was nowhere else to go on her arms. This patient had previously beaten breast cancer. She was lovely, but obviously had a lot on her mind. From memory, she had tried to go to other collection centres, but nobody could find a vein.

The patient told me her blood test was urgent. I tried to find any other vein, but everything else had collapsed. I asked her if I could try her wrist, and she said yes. Her cancer had metastasised and she was going in for surgery on the Monday. It really needed to be done.

I did the blood test, and obviously it was very painful for the patient. It probably wasn't as painful as finding out an aggressive cancer was zapping the life out of a patient, though, so she grunted a little but was quite stoic.

I got her specimen ready, and waited for the courier who was late so the specimen could get to the lab and be tested. I wasn't going to leave it behind. The centre didn't open on the weekend and if the courier hadn't turned up, it would mean the specimen would have been at the centre until the day of the patient's surgery, and I really couldn't have that.

I do think about this patient now and again, and I hope she beat the cancer again.

The woman with leukaemia

I am assuming that most people would think only children are diagnosed with leukaemia. That's what used to be on TV ads for quite some time, when charities asked for donations. Older people can be diagnosed with leukaemia, as well.

I was doing an afternoon shift when an older woman came in. She had been diagnosed with leukaemia a short while previously, so the doctors were keeping a very close eye on her white blood cell count.

During one of her visits to the centre, there was a mishap with one of her most important blood tests. The lab hadn't gotten the results to the specialist in time and they were demanding to know what the results were. The patient had come into the room, and it was a period of time when I was able to get the results sent to the collection centre email to give to her, as the doctor had requested for a copy of the results to be sent to her. I did my utmost, and obtained success. The results were finally sent to the mailbox, and I printed them out for her to take with her.

She did quite a few blood tests to check her white blood cell levels. She was very lovely. I was thankfully always able to find a vein on her. I hope she beat her cancer.

The man on immunotherapy

It was in one of the collection centres that was given to me, and every couple of weeks a patient would walk in for his blood tests. He was the type of man for which nothing would bother him. He also had incredible and very easy veins.

He told me parts about his life, and how he was still working. In fact, his phone never stopped ringing. He had to explain to his staff how to do their jobs. At no stage did he tell them exactly where he was. He just kept going as if he was out for a different type of appointment rather than a medical procedure.

He then told me the type of cancer he had - asbestosis. Also, from memory the immunotherapy appeared not to be working like it had previously, so they put him on chemotherapy. After the first round of chemotherapy, he had told me he was ill but still enjoyed eating chicken.

After a couple of sessions on chemotherapy, he told me he didn't feel much of anything to bother him. He just went on with life as if it was nothing.

The doctor

It was very early on in my career when a doctor found out they were diagnosed with cancer. They knew exactly what was going to happen. Even though they had wonderful veins, they kept insisting on having a blue butterfly needle - the smallest needle in our repertoire.

I saw them a few times, and each and every time I complied. The doctor knew what was going to happen at every step of the way, and I was not going to argue with that.

Doctors live in the communities as people, and they can get sick too. Good doctors are very hard to come by, and this person was a really good doctor who was greatly respected.

The patient with the mask

Patients with a cancer diagnosis rarely ever go in the early morning. The expectation is that the collection centre is crowded early in the morning with everyone who needs to fast. I typically see cancer patients in the mid morning to early afternoon, when there's usually the ability for seating space.

This patient came to me always wearing a mask. I offered some masks to her so she could always be protected, so she wore them everywhere. I also used a butterfly needle on her to keep her vein going so it wouldn't collapse in the future.

I made quite a few suggestions to her initially, not just about wearing masks but also demanding a butterfly wherever she went. I told her if there were no butterflies or there was a refusal, to go elsewhere. Usually, cancer patients can have that one wonderful vein, so keeping the vein going should be the aim for after chemotherapy has concluded.

Whenever she came in, I also ensured that her blood tests were marked as urgent. I wrote the date of each chemotherapy session on the form so the specialist would receive the results before the session.

The patient and her husband were very appreciative of the efforts I made to ensure everything went well. She told me that she did feel unwell after her chemotherapy, but she knew that was to be expected.

Chapter 4 - Patients with autoimmune conditions

As I have been diagnosed with autoimmune conditions, I relate very strongly with the patients who are diagnosed with autoimmune conditions that I do blood tests on. These patients have regular blood tests, as some of the medications can cause liver and kidney problems. Rheumatologists need to monitor the reactions within the body very closely.

There are more autoimmune conditions than can ever be imagined. I have been diagnosed with one, and there's the possibility that another condition will soon be diagnosed as autoimmune but the small community I am part of is waiting to see if an upgrade will occur.

We all have our favourite rheumatologists who look after us. As the specialty is quite small, there are only a few rheumatologists within the community that we depend upon.

The scleroderma patient

This patient has recently become a favourite of mine. She has one very deep vein. She told me once that very few can hit that vein with success. I am fortunate to be one of the few.

The one thing about scleroderma patients is because their body is literally turning into stone, one cannot find anything in the hands. All of them have the coldest hands imaginable, due to Reynaud's disease. This is a condition that turns the hands a different colour due to problems with circulation. The arms are the only places that one can find a vein, and sometimes it becomes too difficult if the scleroderma has become too advanced. I have previously suggested for those patients to go to the hospital, as they have the technology that a typical centre doesn't.

This patient has had scleroderma for many years. She was on similar medication to me, and it was very helpful for her to live a relatively normal life. We have had great conversations in the past about our lives, and how difficult it is to be diagnosed with an autoimmune condition.

She had another vein, but it could be extremely difficult to get anything from it, so I didn't bother trying. She once compared me with another fantastic phlebotomist who no longer lives in the area. That was a really nice compliment.

Another scleroderma patient

I am not successful with blood tests all the time. While we do need a high accuracy rate, sometimes some phlebotomists can find a vein better for some patients than other phlebotomists. I have found that patients pick their favourite phlebotomists. It's not the other way around. It's whoever makes them feel the most comfortable.

A patient came into a really busy centre looking to get her blood test done. She told me from the start that it was extremely difficult to obtain any type of specimen as she had scleroderma. I was warned. I did my utmost to find something. The scleroderma had reached more than halfway up her arms. Everywhere felt hard. Her hands gave absolutely no joy.

She showed me a vein that usually brings some level of success. I used a blue butterfly on it to try to give me something. Unfortunately, the blood stopped before getting into the tube, and then turned hard. Nothing would go into the tube no matter how hard I tried to get at least something in it.

The patient told me this sometimes happened. She said sometimes she would have to go to hospital so a machine could be used for a successful blood test. I recommended she do that, and she started looking as if she was going to cry. She also had Sjögren's syndrome, so crying was difficult for her.

Her scleroderma had become really obvious. I suggested she always go to the hospital for blood tests. We simply didn't have the type of machinery that could help her.

The patients with psoriatic arthritis

Quite a few patients come in for their regular blood tests due to the medications for psoriatic arthritis. As this is one of my autoimmune conditions, I have an enormous amount in common with these patients. They have given me very handy hints, and I have given them solidarity.

One patient told me she was alone with her condition. She had no family or friends who understood the trials and tribulations of psoriatic arthritis. She had a fantastic rheumatologist. When I told her that I also had the condition, she was overjoyed to know that she wasn't alone.

Another patient explained how she had to have hip repair surgery because of the psoriatic arthritis, prior to her being diagnosed with it. Psoriatic arthritis in particular is extremely difficult to diagnose. It doesn't come up in the general blood tests used for autoimmune conditions. A lot of damage can be done to the body before diagnosis.

For me, as a patient, the condition is hereditary. Many of my family members also have psoriatic arthritis, so eventually I was able to be diagnosed before the damage destroyed my hands and feet permanently.

The patients with rheumatoid arthritis

Rheumatoid arthritis is a very debilitating disease that usually starts with the hands. The joints are very painful, and after many years the hands look gnarled.

More than a few patients have walked in to get their blood tests done, after being on medications to reduce the inflammation so they could live a normal life. As it is usually a hereditary autoimmune condition, I tended to ask which family member they got it from to start the conversation. Typically it would be a direct family member, although it could have been a grandparent.

Rheumatoid arthritis is found with a blood test, making it much easier to find diagnosis than with other autoimmune conditions. The medications patients are put on are the same as for other autoimmune conditions, ensuring that I have enough in common with them to ensure good conversations.

The one thing I have noticed is that the younger a person is that is diagnosed, the less one can tell with their hands. One can see the damage rheumatoid arthritis does with the hands when a patient is much older.

The patient with Crohn's disease

Once in a while a patient came in who has been diagnosed with Crohn's disease. Once again, I can relate to this patient as a family member has Crohn's disease. There are now particular tests that can be used to find Crohn's, but when my family member was diagnosed there was nothing other than an unusual X-ray.

As Crohn's disease is an autoimmune condition relating to the lower digestive system, one of the best tests is a faeces test. People with Crohn's disease need to do this test regularly to see if the medication they are on is working. There are also blood tests to ensure that food is be digested properly.

Crohn's disease is a bit of an unusual disease. Patients can all of a sudden have a desperate need to go to the toilet. When that happens, they must drop everything and go, no matter where they are or what they are doing.

This patient needed to do the faeces test in the bathroom of the collection centre. Since the collection centre was very large and not attached to a medical centre, the patient was able to be secure in the knowledge that there would be privacy. Knowing Crohn's disease, I knew that to refuse would have been wrong so I gave them the jar and let them do the specimen. They also had a blood test.

I learned their history of Crohn's disease at the time, and found that the medications worked for this patient. They were able to go about their day with less threat of having to drop everything.

Chapter 5 - Men

There are so many stories about men in the chair, I will try to give only a few. Every patient is vulnerable, but some reactions can be quite perplexing. There are some quite hilarious reactions, because of the way I sometimes look at and talk to the vein and the needle.

The man with the large vein

This was quite early on in my career, in a centre that at the time had poor air conditioning. A patient walked into the room and I went through all the details. I then looked at the vein so I could determine which needle would be the best.

His vein was massive! I could have thrown the needle across the room and hit it perfectly. It barely required any skill to complete the procedure. Sometimes, it's a relief to see a vein as good as this one was.

So I exclaimed 'it's so big!'. The patient then asked 'can you please tell my wife that?'.

As I was talking about the vein instead of anything else in or out of proportion, I declined. I'm guessing his wife would not have been impressed with him if she was there.

The man with the not so large vein

Men can have quite a dirty comedic mind. This story comes from a more recent experience.

The patient walked into the room for a blood test. I checked his vein, and it was a typical size that I see quite often. Easy to get to, and easy enough for me to obtain all necessary specimens.

The patient then asked 'isn't my vein just the largest you've ever seen? My vein is quite large' And I replied 'it's not as big as some that I've seen before'. His response? 'That's what all my previous girlfriends have said'. I loudly exclaimed 'you're married!'.

He was quite jovial with the experience. Anyone who took him seriously during that episode would probably have been quite offended. As it was, I see so many different people that I shrugged it off as if it was nothing but a quaint little story to once in a while tell people.

The man with dementia

For a while, I was in a room only in the mornings. A man walked in with his father who had dementia. At all times, I had to ask the son all details as he had power of attorney over his father. The father understood very little of what was going on.

He had brought his son up to be a good man before the dementia had obviously hit him. The son didn't just look out for his father. He also looked out for me.

While I was doing the father's blood test, the father started trying to grope me. He tried as many times as he could, until the son found out what he was doing and kept telling him to stop it. The father was successful at touching my crotch once, and my buttocks once as they were walking out of the room.

Dealing with people who have dementia is complex. As the son was telling his father to stop touching me, I saw no need to take it further, or to complain. The son was doing his best to curb his father's behaviour on his own, and I didn't want to complicate things or make life harder for the son.

The man with his daughter

Early on in my career, while I was moving around a lot, I was in a room that had many elderly patients. It was a lovely quiet area, and many people had retired to this area to relax during their retirement years.

It was in this room that a patient came in with his daughter. I went through all the particulars, and then checked his vein. For some reason, I felt that the patient and his daughter didn't want to talk, so I didn't start up a conversation. The daughter then said that she was relieved, as she couldn't stand it when people kept talking while doing her father's blood test.

I am a very cheeky person. As soon as someone has said this, I have started talking about my cat. The main reason for this is because the person started complaining about other phlebotomists. They complained about how the phlebotomist talked too much about their personal life, or wouldn't shut up. It's my way of showing that we are all human, too.

I finally completed the blood test, and they went on their way.

The extremely grumpy old man

From my experience, the older a man gets, the less patience he has with everyone. I have had a few experiences with grumpy old men, but this one stands out in particular.

It was the first day of school and I was a relief. So many phlebotomists had called in sick, I ended up being mostly by myself in a room where there should have been at least 2 phlebotomists. There was a trainee for a small window of time, but not in the afternoon for which I had by that time become exhausted.

I had a bit of relief for a short time, and had to lock the door so I could have lunch. So many people walked through that door on that day. I had a lot of difficulty keeping up.

It was towards the end of my shift, when 3 patients walked through the door. One woman needed to do a urine sample, so I let her do it, and then catered to the next patient in the room. The woman had come back, so I did her blood test.

The last patient was the elderly grumpy old man. He had to wait, because the other patients had come in first. I sorted everything out and finished the blood test, and as he was leaving he loudly said to the room full of patients 'that was the longest time I've ever had to wait for a blood test'.

I was infuriated and humiliated. I guess that was his intent. He had offered to wait, as well, and then he decided to humiliate me in front of others. It wasn't a good experience.

The man with the easy vein

A while ago, when I had a permanent afternoon shift, a patient walked into the room for a blood test. I had had a very long day and most of my previous patients had very difficult veins.

This patient had a very easy vein. I was probably a little tired at the time, but upon seeing the vein I started saying how successful I was with *all* the difficult veins on patients and how relieved I was that he had such an easy vein. I'm not sure what he thought, but at that time I assumed that as it was an easy vein I would get it first time.

I missed!

I wasn't the only one surprised. While I was trying again, and that time being successful, he told me that it was the first time anyone had missed his veins. I decided not to act quite so confident ever again after that.

While we do need a certain level of confidence, saying it out loud could mean that one may not be as successful as they would like to be. I definitely learned my lesson that time!

The firefighter

It was a very busy centre that usually had a minimum of 2 phlebotomists in it. My coworker had gone to lunch, and while she was away a firefighter walked through the door. It was winter, and the clothing he wore was not appropriate for having a blood test.

I was the lucky one to do this patient's blood test. He told me that he was in one of the calendars, and I would believe it. I asked him to take his arm out of his sleeve so I could gain access to his arm for the blood test.

Instead, he took his top off. I was very happy.

He was very easy on the eyes. As a much older woman, I had no qualms in telling him that. He told me he was blushing, but he definitely liked the attention. I said nothing more than that, and kept everything professional. He promised to ask his coworkers to come in for their blood tests and I told him the best times to do so. Saturdays were far too busy to bring a fire truck into the parking area!

While he was leaving, my coworker came back from lunch. She saw him and asked what happened. I told her I just did his blood test and he took his top off. She demanded to know why I didn't wait for her to return because she wanted to do his blood test instead. I told her tough luck, better luck next time. Plus, she was married.

The man who called me a vampire

It was when we all had to wear masks outside as a prerequisite. I was in the smallest room imaginable, and had to let the patient into the room first.

It's very hard to see facial features when one is wearing a mask. Just before the patient walked in the door before me, he asked me if I liked being called a vampire. I smiled, as that's exactly how I introduced myself at the time. He couldn't see my smile so assumed the worst.

He then asked if I was offended. I lowered my mask to show my smile, and then put my mask back on again. I then told him that was how I saw myself. He smiled, and then sat on the chair.

The man who didn't drink any water

More often than not, when a doctor tells a patient to fast they usually come in not having had anything touch their lips. Water is actually acceptable, and a patient can have a few glasses without having their results affected. There are a couple of stories about men who think they are macho by not drinking water. This is very unhelpful, and they find out in the bleeding chair exactly how unhelpful and painful it can be.

With this one particular story, the man came in for a blood test in a recent collection centre. At the time, I had just recovered from illness so hadn't known that he had also come in while I was away. I found his vein with difficulty. It felt very flat.

I had asked him if he had drunk any water. He said he hadn't had anything since the night before. I asked him how much water he drinks throughout the day, and he said much less than a litre per day every day.

I started the blood test, and got very little in one tube but needed another. By this time, his vein had completely dried up. There was nothing left and he was *very* dehydrated. He was also in severe pain. I couldn't get anything more out of him because there was nothing left in him.

He then told me that he had another blood test while I was away, and that one was very painful as well. I knew the phlebotomist who did that blood test, and found she could only get a minimal amount. It was all because he didn't want to drink water.

I stopped the blood test and asked him to come back for the rest after he had hydrated at another time. I then explained how a person's red blood cells are made, and that the only way for blood cells to go through the body was with water. Water is the main carrier of all cells and nutrients throughout the whole body, and one needs water every day to ensure that everything works properly.

A few months later, he came back for another blood test. I asked him if he had drunk water, and he said he had. His vein felt as if he had drunk water, and the blood test was one of the least painful he had ever had. He learned his lesson.

The man with the prostate blood test

The prostate blood test is one of the more frustrating tests that phlebotomists do. The reason is not the test itself. It is a very easy blood test. The frustration lies in all the conditions surrounding the test.

Government policies affect the community every day. While government do their thing in the hope of saving a few dollars here and there, it can adversely affect what happens to a person, and whether they have to pay for something that I believe should be on Medicare in its entirety. Men should not have to be charged to check to see if they have prostate cancer, or even inflammation or enlargement of their prostate. Yet they sometimes do.

There are conditions that need to be met on a man's prostate blood test. The only way for a doctor to diagnose a man for any prostate condition is to have several consecutive prostate blood tests over a short period of time. During a 2 year period and if not diagnosed or with no family history, only one of these tests is on Medicare, and the patient would have to pay for the rest until they are diagnosed. An example of where it could all go wrong is below.

A man walked into a recent collection centre. He had a prostate blood test, and the doctor had probably diagnosed the man with a prostate condition prior to him coming in, for which all his blood tests would have been on Medicare.

I asked him about his prostate conditions and whether he was diagnosed. I had to ask about his conditions. He said he wasn't diagnosed with anything.

I asked him when he had his last prostate blood test. He told me it was recently. I knew there was something up. I kept telling him that he would be charged because it wouldn't be on Medicare unless he was diagnosed. He told me his doctor hadn't told him anything, and he had difficulty talking with his doctor about certain issues. He still kept saying he wasn't diagnosed with anything, nor did he have a family history.

There are many times when a man doesn't want to tell a phlebotomist that there's a problem with his health. He probably feels embarrassed and has the assumption that he's no longer invincible. These are the times when I get frustrated with government officials who, to me, are playing with people's health. To us, it's a job that we have to do.

I finally got the information from this patient by prodding him. I had to ask about his symptoms and he finally told me he had prostate symptoms. I guessed that his doctor *had* diagnosed him with a prostate condition, but his embarrassment had told him to reject every question I had asked him about his health.

These are the times when I dearly wished that the government minister for health would be in the same room to see how their decisions adversely affect the whole country. I have emailed and called certain ministers and envoys, yet there's still these conditions put onto men's health that adversely affect them.

Chapter 6 - Women

I have had regulars come in, telling me how much they loved it when I was successful with their vein first go. This doesn't happen all the time. Other collectors have been better than I could be with some patients. We all have different skills, and are not afraid to ask a patient to go elsewhere when the need arises. Women in general don't behave as emotionally towards blood tests as men do. These are some stories of women having their blood tests done.

The woman with the wriggliest veins ever

When I first started learning the job, I had an incredible mentor. She showed me aspects of the job that helped me become nearly as successful as she was. She had worked for several years in the job so knew all the tricks. One trick was to tamp down the wriggly veins on each side of the vein so putting the needle in would be much more successful. She told me it was not quite an acceptable method because there could be more likelihood of a needle injury, but it was extremely effective.

At a very busy afternoon centre, a patient with very major health concerns needed a blood test. She was extremely reluctant to have blood tests as very few people could get anything from her veins. These veins stuck out like a sore thumb. They were absolutely massive, but whenever a phlebotomist went anywhere near them they would jump around and the phlebotomist would miss.

She had a vein on both arms like that, but I always decided to do her left arm. It was bigger, even though it was even wrigglier. Each and every time she came into the centre for a blood test, she would be relieved because I could obtain something by using my old mentor's trick.

At that time, she was about to have major surgery that was quite urgent at the time. One of her tests kept being abnormal, so doctors would put off the surgery until the test was normal, which meant she needed to have many blood tests over the course of several weeks.

Each time she came in, she would be crying over the pain and frustration. She would be very appreciative that I was able to do her blood test with minimal pain, but the pain before surgery was too much for her. At least that one thing kept going right for her.

Finally, she was given the go ahead for surgery. There were complications arising from the surgery, but they were rectified at a later date.

The woman who hadn't drunk any water

This was a while ago, in a daytime collection centre. A patient walked into the room for a blood test. I checked everything, and then asked if the patient had drunk any water. She said she never drank water, and she actually hated drinking water without anything else in it. She much preferred to drink coffee.

I then told her what happens in relation to how water carries blood cells and nutrients throughout the body. She was still determined to go without water. Coffee was her favourite drink and she refused nearly anything else. She also said it was sometimes hard for phlebotomists to find a vein.

Sometimes phlebotomists can hit and miss with the same patients with consecutive blood tests. Sometimes the vein is easy to find, and other times it can be difficult. It's up to the time of day, as well as how the patient is feeling and also how the phlebotomist is feeling. When a patient is unwell, it can be more difficult to find much of anything.

The first time I did this patient's blood test, I was successful. It went slowly, but that was because of the lack of water. I was surprised, but happy. That was when she told me she refused to drink water.

Because I was successful the first time, she tried her luck with me again for a second time. That time, I was unsuccessful. Her lack of water produced literally nothing. There wasn't much I could do, other than suggest she go elsewhere to another phlebotomist.

The regulars who always have a smile

I actually have many stories of regulars who come in with a smile when they see me. They brighten my world, and keep me in the job when I question my life's priorities or have a really hard day. These regulars are generally women, although some men are also regulars and also smile when they see me.

Usually, the regular patients have to be monitored by their doctor or specialist for conditions that can be quite complex. One regular had a really nice vein, but I still preferred to use a butterfly needle on her because her vein was being used regularly. She was always very friendly, and was older. She once told me that the reason why she continually came around was not just because she lived close to the centre, but also because I'm friendly.

Another younger patient came in regularly as her doctor didn't know what condition she had at the time. She told me she liked for me to do her blood test as she was a difficult bleed and I didn't bruise her quite as much as she had unfortunately been bruised beforehand.

Another patient came from far away. She was pregnant and had to lie down for her blood tests, which could only be successful in her hand. I offered jelly beans to her each time, which she loved because she knew she can drive soon afterwards.

The patient who thought I'd recognise her

Phlebotomists don't know from day to day whether the room is going to be empty or crowded with standing room only. There are a few collection centres that are always extremely busy, and expected to be busy at all times. Some of those rooms have 2 phlebotomists, and some of the rooms have only 1 phlebotomist who is very experienced.

There have been times when patients came in and out rather quickly, but it depended on what the doctor wanted. Some specimens require a lot of work in the background.

In a recent room a short while ago, on this day the waiting room was quite busy. It was a day where extra requirements for some specimens had to be made. I had finally nearly cleared the waiting room and there were 3 patients left. One woman stands up and says 'do you remember me?' I said 'no', because I barely remember anyone.

She said 'you did my blood test a few months ago, and you let me stay lying down for 5 minutes after the blood test'. I told her I still didn't remember her, but I would be letting her lie down for 5 minutes afterwards this time too.

She was the last patient of the rush, so when she finally came in she said how she couldn't believe that I didn't remember her. I actually can't remember anyone. I make it a point to forget names and faces as soon as the patient walked out the door. It helps maintain privacy. I told her that, and she understood.

As with many people, she had trauma with previous experiences from when she was a child. I did what I could to distract her while she was lying down, and was successful very quickly with obtaining the sample. I then let her stay lying down, and offered the jelly beans. She loved that experience, and didn't quite need the whole 5 minutes.

The woman with the vein close to the armpit

I was in an extremely busy centre when a very frustrated patient walked in. She had come from another centre, and while the phlebotomist had been very close to the vein, they hadn't wriggled it around a bit so unfortunately had missed the vein. As per procedure, they had to tell the patient to go elsewhere, so the patient came to me.

Sometimes veins can appear to feel very good, but they make a laughing stock of us in that the area is deceptive. There's nobody to blame for that. It is what it is.

I tried one area that looked good and was somewhat near where the other phlebotomist had been. It was a failure.

I then tried nearly exactly where the other phlebotomist had been. It was nearly like a landmark, and right near the armpit. The patient told me to try there and move it around. All of a sudden, I got a jackpot in one of the most unusual places for a vein that I'd ever seen. It didn't even look like a place one could go.

The patient was very grateful at how determined I was. She told me very few people could get to her veins, and she was extremely frustrated each and every time a doctor wanted her to go for a blood test. She only went when it was a last resort, because of how many times phlebotomists were forced to tell her to go elsewhere.

The woman with the surface vein

This was several months into my career, and I was working with a mentor I fully respected. A woman came into the centre in tears. She was told to go elsewhere and ended up in pain. It seriously was nobody's fault. She was extremely difficult and had an urgent blood test.

I tried and failed. I had also brought her to tears, and I couldn't find anywhere on her arms or hands. At that point, I asked my mentor to help me.

She had enormous experience in the job, and all she could find was a surface vein the patient's arm. She decided to try there, and found success. She showed me how to get surface veins and how to be careful when doing so.

Even now, when I do surface veins, I can have mixed success. They are some of the trickiest veins to obtain anything from, and anything could go wrong in the process.

The extremely difficult bleed

This story is from various different collection centres. It was almost as if this patient kept accidentally finding me.

A patient with a very thin vein came into the collection centre. I decided to use a butterfly needle for her. It went at an unusual angle, in her arm.

This patient had complained about how difficult it was to find a phlebotomist who could extract anything from her. Usually, she would end up with bruises everywhere. Not much could have been done by this, as it was nobody's fault. It just was, and the patient knew it but still had a rough time. In addition to this, she needed regular blood tests because she had autoimmune diseases.

Each and every time I saw her, I was successful. She ended up being very happy to see me, and I used a butterfly needle nearly each and every time.

Apart from one time. I was doing an afternoon shift in a centre, and she came in with her children. They all needed to have blood tests. The children were easy to obtain anything, so they went first. Then it was her turn. There were no butterfly needles left in the entirety of the centre. I offered to turn her away, but she refused.

So I used what we classify as 'flash' needles. These are needles that have a little window in them, to guarantee success if we hit a vein. They are a necessity in all collection centres and also help with very deep veins.

I was successful that time, but it was a very slow process. Anything could have happened to dislodge the needle from the vein. It was a very tricky procedure.

The patient then said 'see, I knew you could do it'. It was quite a relief.

The extremely deep vein

In a recent centre, a young woman came in with her mother. The young woman had had difficulty for the majority of her life with successful blood tests. She was very relaxed about the procedure, but knew it could be frustrating to find anything.

Neither the patient nor her mother told me that she had problems with blood tests. Once in a while, a patient won't say anything with the hope that any vein would finally work for them. This was one of those times.

I felt for a vein and took my time. I finally found something, but it was extremely deep. It needed a flash needle, not just to know if I was successful but also because this needle was longer than all the other needles that I had in my repertoire.

I then went in, and had to do a small amount of fishing, but found it and it was a really good vein. It took most of the length of this very long needle to obtain anything. I was able to obtain the full amount required.

Both the mother and daughter were surprised, and very happy. I explained how I was able to obtain the specimens, and suggested that they could explain this to others if they needed a blood test with other phlebotomists. I also suggested for them to get a tattoo of the general area so nobody had to miss again.

The woman a doctor was very concerned about

I was in a centre that was unusually busy, within a medical centre. I was asked to do a blood test on a woman who was visiting from overseas. It appeared there may have been heart problems, and the doctor begged me to do a blood test on the woman. She was lying down in the medical centre treatment room.

She was unable to get up. It appeared that she collapsed within the medical centre so the doctor was quite frantic.

I had to first get all her details as per the form. The daughter was of great help in relation to that. She had all the details and ensured her mother's private health insurance was written on the form. I then got all the equipment ready to do the blood test.

Unfortunately, the first time I tried I failed to get any sample. It was utterly crucial that I obtain something and the pressure was definitely on, so I went back into my room and got another butterfly needle to use on the patient. I was successful, but only just.

These types of situations usually give us a bit more anxiety than usual. We are here to help find results, and sometimes the pressure to do well can be enormous.

Chapter 7 - Children

Children require much more skill when it comes to blood tests. We need to ensure there is the minimum trauma made onto children as possible, although more often than not we are not successful and the child screams out in pain. The first day that I was signed off to be on my own, I was sent to a collection centre and one of the patients was a 9 year old girl. When it comes to patients who are children, practice makes perfect, but the practice needs to cause the least pain possible.

The little girl with the father

I had been working a several months, and was put in a centre that had an afternoon shift. A father walked in with his very small daughter. He had put numbing cream onto her arms and wrapped plastic wrap around the areas.

Unfortunately, all he put on her arms was a little dot in the middle that hadn't covered nearly enough of the area that was required. It missed the best vein the little girl had.

It was definitely a learning moment for the father. The little girl screamed while I obtained the bare minimum that I could. She was very unhappy with the experience. The father held her with an iron grip the whole time, but I could tell he was also quite traumatised by the experience.

I showed him the vein for the next time, and asked him to cover the whole area so she didn't have to suffer ever again. I also told him to keep the numbing cream on the arm and wrapped in plastic for one hour before coming into any collection centre. That way, the child would feel nothing for the whole procedure.

The teenage boy

Teenagers can be worse than adults or younger children when it comes to blood tests. This boy certainly proved it.

He was very tall - much taller than his mother. I had done his mothers blood tests previously, and she knew what to expect. She liked coming to me, so wanted me to do her son's blood tests. She was there with him throughout the whole procedure. She had put numbing cream on his arms, and kept it on for an hour with plastic wrap.

To say he was nervous was an understatement! It took a while for us to coax him onto the chair. It took a while longer to get him ready to get near to having the blood test. The thought of having a blood test terrified him, so I used a butterfly needle and told him that it wasn't going to hurt. I had assumed the numbing cream would have worked by that time.

It really didn't matter. The mother held her son's head and tried to distract him. We both told him to keep his arm still. He still screamed the whole medical centre down. Everyone in the building heard his screams.

Afterwards, he calmed down and I finished all the paperwork. As they were leaving the room, he said 'I'm never going to have another blood test ever again!'. I replied 'this is just the start and you're going to have blood tests for the rest of your life so you'd better get used to them'. His mother laughed, while he looked utterly crestfallen.

The girl with the grandmother

A grandmother walked into a busy afternoon centre with her little granddaughter who was the patient. The girl was very respectful, but was very reluctant to have a blood test. Usually, I get the blood test over and done with first when it comes to children, so their fear is dramatically reduced. I ask all details on the form verbally, and then get to the blood test straight away.

The girl started crying, and the grandmother told me that one of her most recent blood tests was very traumatic for her and she had memories of how bad it was. Sometimes, especially if someone hasn't drunk enough water, this can happen.

The grandmother was on one side of the girl, ensuring that the girl looked at her rather than at what I was doing. She was telling stories about different times in their lives that were positive to try to distract her.

I had found an easy vein and got to work with getting the required amounts for the 2 tubes that I needed. The girl was still crying, and as I changed to the second tube the girl asked 'is it in yet?'.

That was a massive compliment. The girl had no idea I was nearly finished with the blood test until her grandmother said 'she's nearly finished' and laughed at the response of her little girl being utterly surprised. The tears ended very quickly after that.

Both the grandmother and the little girl were very impressed. By this time, I had the tendency to buy jelly beans for children (and myself when I got hungry). I offered a jelly bean to the girl while finishing up all the paperwork.

By this experience, I hoped the girl had a much better memory for her next blood test.

The boy who got dizzy

As this is typically a new experience for children, they can get extremely nervous and their behaviour can become understandably erratic. They can hyperventilate. They usually don't eat or drink anything because their nervousness gets in the way.

A boy with his mother came into a very busy centre. It was the boy's first time, and he was quite dehydrated. The mother was really helpful and very caring. It wasn't that she refused to give him anything. It was a case that this poor boy refused it as he had way too many butterflies in his stomach from nervous anticipation.

I completed the blood test, after giving appropriate instructions to make him look at his mother the entire time and get him talking to his mother to distract him. It was a successful blood test. Then, he started saying he felt dizzy.

Straight away, I gave him water. He was *really* thirsty. He drank the whole amount. He then exclaimed 'it's like the elixir of life!'. His mother and I said in unison 'well, yeah'. We both told him that because he finally had his blood test, there would be nothing to worry about and he really should drink water from then on. They then went about their day.

The girl who needed to see things differently

In a recent centre, a girl came in with her mother. The girl had already had quite a few traumatic experiences when it cam to blood tests, so was very nervous.

Her mother and I decided to try everything to distract her. She had numbing cream on that was already taken off to try to save time. Her mother was an incredible woman who understood her daughter.

Her mother put her favourite music on, and I tried to dance to it. As I had difficulty moving around due to physical problems, it was difficult and a little painful for me to dance, but I looked like a dork and that was the main reason for it. It was a method to distract the girl.

Her mother and I then tried other methods of distraction. The girl couldn't keep her arm still for the blood test. She was too nervous to go ahead.

So I sat down and waited. The mother kept asking if she wanted to get the blood test done. The girl said yes, but not yet.

Phlebotomists are part of the community. We see all the psychological factors that exist in everyday living. We need to be experts in people in order to do our jobs.

So I asked her the question 'what are you thinking about?'. The girl answered 'pain, that it will hurt'. I told her the numbing cream was on her so she would feel nothing. I touched her arm and asked her if she could feel it. She said no.

A short while later, I asked her again 'what are you thinking about?'. She then said 'blood'. So I told her the trick I had decided to have when I first started my training for the job. I told her to think of it as a red liquid instead of blood, to separate herself from what it was to a different type of liquid that didn't come from the body.

It worked. After that, she was ready and I was able to obtain the entirety of her specimen. She then asked to look at it, and asked for some of the scientific aspects of it, and I happily explained everything to her. I gave her some jelly beans. Both she and her mother told me I was never allowed to leave and they would always come back.

The identical twins

In a recent room, a family waited for me to finish with a previous patient, and then told me both of their sons needed a blood test. Unbeknownst to me, I had already completed a successful blood test with one of the sons, but not the other. I vaguely recall the mother telling me he had an identical twin, but couldn't remember who it was so it was a bit of a surprise to see them.

Both parents were there, and they asked me which boy should have the blood test first. I told them the most nervous boy as it then could be over and done with and he would have known that he survived. They picked one of the boys, and he sat on the chair.

He was very scared. I needed both parents to help me. One parent held his arm so he couldn't pull it away, and the other parent did everything they could to distract him. It didn't quite work, but I was able to obtain a sample eventually. He did cry, until after it was over. I offered him some jelly beans and he eventually got over the experience.

After all the paperwork for the first boy was completed, I then got ready for the second boy. He sat there and accepted the blood test very calmly. It was very easy to obtain a sample from him.

The mother then told the first boy that if he calmed down and accepted it, then the blood test would go much easier. The first boy then understood by looking at his brother.

I then asked the mother 'how do you tell them apart?' She told me that this time, she let them dress themselves. They ended up with identical clothing apart from a t-shirt. One of them had a longer t-shirt than the other. Other than that, every single thing about them was completely identical.

While that conversation was going on, the boys had decided to raid some of the rest of the jelly beans. It was amusing to watch the parents tell them to only take a couple and leave the rest for me.

The little boy who watched

This story was in one of the many afternoon shifts in one of the larger collection centres. A father and his son came into the room, and the son needed to have a blood test. I got all the equipment out. The boy didn't even flinch. There were a few tubes, and he sat there with a look of expectation.

By this time, I assumed that this centre had stickers for children who have blood tests, so I offered the boy a sticker. One of the other phlebotomists was great with children, and I thought she had stickers.

The boy watched the whole procedure. I never like it when anyone watches as I believed everyone assessed me, but he was at his tender age very experienced at having blood tests so he sat there. I remember saying 'oh my, I could have drained him!'. Of course, I stopped at the required specimen and did nothing more.

The boy then asked for his sticker, so I went searching. I looked high and low for these stickers. I went *everywhere*! I couldn't find one single sticker anywhere. The father then said 'don't worry, I'll give him a treat when we leave'. I felt so embarrassed, as I couldn't go through with what I promised.

The young children when I was very new

Most children are very difficult to keep distracted. It was probably during my work experience I found a semi good distraction technique that worked for a short period of time. One of my fabulous mentors told me she just got it over and done with so the child didn't overthink things, and I now also do that.

While I was doing work experience before getting a job with a company, I was helping another phlebotomist out while they were doing the blood test when I said to the child 'did you know that I walk my cat on a leash and harness?'. Before and just after gaining employment children used to get distracted by that. I would then answer questions on how I got an 8 year old cat at the time to walk on a leash and harness.

This technique died off somewhat. Pixie's allure on how I got her to walk around at the age of 8 just didn't have any lustre after a while.

There are now other ways. One child wanted to know everything of scientific value within the room, so I showed what the chemicals within each coloured tube looked like, as well as what happens to each tube when a sample is inside it. I then showed the centrifuge and how it spins the tubes to create the desired effect to obtain a result from the lab.

Another technique for prospective mathematicians is to count the squares of numbers until I have finished. I would ask the young patient what each number squared is. I can give the number up to 15, so it's a good technique for distraction.

Yet another technique is using a child's love of sport. I told one child not to worry, and hopefully one day he would be just as good as the Matildas soccer team when he grew up. He laughed at that.

In essence, I would use the topic the child is most comfortable with to distract the child into being calm enough to obtain a specimen.

Chapter 8 - Patients on blood thinners

Quite regularly, some patients are on blood thinners due to heart or blood clot problems. These patients are regulars. Their results are usually available by the end of the day so their doctor could advise on how much medication to take the next day. Sometimes, the vein has been overused due to how many blood tests over decades a patient needs to have. These patients can have only one vein that phlebotomists can rely upon. Other patients can have more, which is fortunate for them.

The young man

I was working in one of my permanent afternoon shifts in a very busy centre. A young man came in regularly and offered the only vein he had which caused the least amount of pain. It was a relatively easy vein, so there were no problems with obtaining a specimen.

He was a very friendly man, and very accepting of all the blood tests he needed to have to ensure his blood thinners were behaving properly. It was unusual to see someone so young being on a blood thinner. I asked him his history, and he said he was diagnosed very early with blood clots so after treatment he was put on the blood thinner to keep him healthy.

Bad health can come from those least deserving. This man accepted everything that came his way.

The older woman 1

This story is early on in my career, when I was working in a busy centre with one of my favourite coworkers. Even though this coworker has moved on, we still keep in touch. She is *very* experienced and has worked for several years in the industry. Many patients love her and still talk positively about her.

This particular patient also loved her. They have had many conversations together and knew about each other's lives. My coworker had always been able to obtain a successful specimen on the first try.

For me, each and every time I tried I was only ever successful on the second try. When it comes to patients on blood thinners, we need to be careful because it can take a very long period of time for the bleeding to stop. If we are unsuccessful on the first go, then we need to wait quite a while before we can try again.

With this patient, each and every time the blood test would take much longer, and all because I kept missing. I was never sure why I kept missing. It was annoying for me each and every time.

The patient was very kind and kept telling me to try again. She was just as surprised that I kept missing as I was.

The older woman 2

Recently, an older patient came in for her test as she all of a sudden had issues with her blood thinners and the doctors were trying to get it under control again. She was very frustrated, and only had one very scarred vein. This vein still worked. She was very aware that she would be feeling pain with each and every blood test due to all the scarring. It couldn't be helped. Usually, we stay away from scarring but if there's only one working vein we have no choice but to use it.

The patient came in and stated that she used to go to a busier centre but her favourite phlebotomist no longer worked there and she didn't like the phlebotomists who were there. Patients have their favourites. There's nothing wrong with any of the other phlebotomists. It was just people's preferences.

She told me who the phlebotomist was, and I knew instantly that it was one of my favourite coworkers. I told her where she could find this phlebotomist, but also that she was moving on soon so she'd better get there soon. She said she would do that, and after the other phlebotomist had left she would come back to me.

I have done her blood test several times now, and found the least painful way to obtain a successful specimen was to use a blue butterfly on her scarred arm. Once in a while, I caused pain. It was the last thing I wanted to do.

The older woman 3

While I was relieving other phlebotomists, I was rostered to a very busy centre for one day. An older woman came into the centre needing to check her blood thinning medication. I did the blood test, and then waited for an extended period of time to ensure there was no bleeding. We initially waited quite some time for it the bleeding to stop, and when it did I put tape on the area as per normal.

By the time she signed the paperwork, she started bleeding again. She had to sit in the chair for another very extended period of time to ensure it stopped bleeding again. We were both surprised that it didn't stop after the first extended period of time.

The older man

This story is from earlier on in my career. Sometimes the most faithful areas on a patient's arm can all of a sudden run dry. This was one of the times that this has happened.

A patient walked into a very busy centre needing his blood thinner test. I tried the place where he said to go, and it came up with… nothing. This was at a time when we could try a few times. He really needed the blood test because his medication was changing. I tried elsewhere… still nothing.

So I checked his hands, and those hands had the biggest veins imaginable!

I asked to go in his hand instead. He agreed, as long as I didn't hurt him in the arm again. I tried his hand and it was very successful.

Once in a while, if the arms give us nothing it's worthwhile checking the hands. I have converted more than a few to use their hands because it can be less painful then trying to dig around in the arm and causing immense pain. This patient was converted.

The next time he came into this centre, he offered his hand. He decided to get his blood tests done from the hand at all times in the future.

The woman with the extremely difficult bleed

I was in one of my morning centres. About mid morning, a woman came into the room claiming she was extremely difficult. She needed to get her blood thinning medication done, as well as some other tests.

I tried to find at least something, and found a vein in her hand. It was one of the most difficult blood tests I had ever done to that moment, but I did get a sample. It was slow going, as well.

Unfortunately, the lab had a problem with the specimen. It had coagulated before getting to the lab. This sometimes happens.

So the woman had to have the blood test again, although by that time I had moved elsewhere so another phlebotomist had to try to find a vein on this poor woman.

Chapter 9 - Patients with troponin

Some blood samples are so urgent, a taxi has to be called to transport the patient's specimens to the lab. There are a few, and all phlebotomists know exactly which ones they are. Sometimes, the patient comes for their blood test at the busiest of times, and phlebotomists have to roll with the times and accept that we will be running a bit behind due to calling the lab for a taxi to transport these tests.

The time I forgot

It was during one of my afternoon shifts and I was very busy. A patient came in with a troponin and D-dimer test. Both of those were urgent, but one infinitely more urgent than the other. I was so swamped with patients, and from memory this patient also needed to have a urine test.

So I did the blood test, and then asked them to straight away do the urine. Then I went to the next patient… and the next patient… and the next patient.

A short while later, I received a phone call. It was nearing the hour which was the period of time where the lab needed the specimen, and I forgot to make the crucial phone call to the lab to call for a taxi.

I apologised profusely. Time had gotten away from me, and I had actually told the patient to expect a phone call within 2 hours for the results. That wasn't about to happen in time if the specimen wasn't even there.

A taxi was called at that time, and the specimen got to the lab shortly after the required time. I haven't forgotten again due to that one incident.

The taxi that got lost

There is a 4 hour window to get some specimens to the lab. If the courier is late, then a taxi needs to be called to take the specimen to the lab. Phlebotomists need to calculate the amount of time to see whether a taxi should be called. I was doing a busy afternoon shift, and I found out that the usual courier was away, with a relief filling in.

I had contacted the lab and requested for a taxi for a specimen that had a 4 hour window to get to the lab, because something within me assumed that the courier would be late. The lab told me not to worry and the courier would come within the window of time open for this specimen.

It was getting late and there was still no courier. I contacted the lab several times wondering where the courier was. I was freaking out by this stage as the time limit was coming up, so the lab called for a taxi to come and pick the specimen up.

By the time my shift nearly ended, the taxi still hadn't turned up and nor had the courier. Neither appeared to be getting anywhere near where I was. I called the lab yet again, and waited in an open area with some kind of expectation that at least one of them would arrive soon. At that point in time, I was still on the phone with the lab when they told me the taxi had gone to another centre and then stopped close by but not close enough to pick up any specimens.

Eventually, the taxi walked from a distance to obtain the specimen. The driver had gotten so lost, he had no idea where exactly to go so he stopped and walked to try to find the entrance. He finally found me and collected the parcel with the specimen in it.

The courier finally came shortly before I finished my shift. By that time, all other specimens were in the special box outside the centre and I was cleaning up for the day. The courier asked where the specimens were and I told them.

That was definitely a very stressful afternoon.

The many troponin tests for the one patient

I was in a daytime centre and a patient walked into the room. He had told me that he had just gotten out of hospital and the specialists were going to need to check his troponin levels over an extended period of time.

This patient was one of the nicest men I had ever known. Initially he was quite concerned. He had many health concerns and needed to be monitored closely.

He asked me what the best time was for getting a blood test close to the time when the courier turned up that wouldn't be very busy. I told him the time, and each day he needed the test done I would see him in the centre. It was like clockwork.

Once in a while, the patient would come much earlier, I called the lab asking for a taxi. This happened only a few times, but after the patient had had his troponin blood test it was found that the specialist didn't need the results quite so urgently. Even though troponin was an urgent blood test, this particular specimen could reach the lab with the normal courier, no matter how much time had passed.

The troponin at the end of the shift

I was well into my career and doing an afternoon shift in a very busy centre. I had a few latecomers shortly before my shift ended. Sometimes, the rush came late on a Friday afternoon. One of the reasons for that was because on Saturdays, people were off work and the rush could be extreme.

On this particular day, a patient came in complaining of chest pain. There were other patients before and after him, but I knew his specimen was extremely urgent. I called the lab requesting for taxi pickup of the specimen. Then I finished all other patients in the waiting room.

After a while, the taxi hadn't come. I contacted the lab again, and was told that the taxi company had cancelled the request. They offered to contact the taxi company again for another taxi. That one was outright rejected. Another taxi then also cancelled.

As I was close enough to the lab, I told the lab that I wasn't going to wait around for another taxi rejection so I offered to take all the specimens to the lab. They agreed. It was going to be the only way to get the specimen to the lab.

I ended up being later than the required hour, but the lab was aware that the specimens were coming and gave alleviation for the time difference. Thankfully, I was paid overtime for the extended period of work, and then I went home.

There are times when phlebotomists go out of their way for the patients. This was one of those times.

Chapter 10 - Complicated samples

There are a number of specimens that have very complicated administrative requirements after a patient has left. More often than not, these specimens need to be put in the freezer overnight and sent to the lab frozen. Some also need to be wrapped in aluminium foil as light disintegrates the test.

As these specimens require an enormous amount of work, phlebotomists can be a little late for the patients in the waiting room. Usually, after the patient has left, I walk into the waiting room and say 'that was a very long test!', hoping to make light of the amount of time I needed for the prior patient.

Gastric band surgery

Quite a few patients walk into a centre prior to surgery to reduce their stomach. Judgment is rife within the community, and more often than not a patient will feel the need to have the surgery because they feel that they have no other option. There also may be a medical reason for the surgery, and as I'm not a doctor I will never be one to judge.

There isn't a story of one particular patient. They all have most of the tests in common, and some patients need to lie down because of how many tubes are necessary for their specimen.

The tests mostly in common are checking for vitamin levels. Phlebotomists need to know, or be aware of, which vitamins are in the general mix and which vitamins have specialised procedures. For that, we have an easy to read manual where we can search for the test prior to starting the blood test. This manual can be found online with all pathology organisations.

The tests we generally see the most often for gastric band surgery are vitamin A, vitamin E, vitamin B1, vitamin B6, vitamin B12 and vitamin D. Once in a while, we will see other vitamins thrown into the mix, such as vitamin C and vitamin K. Those are such unusual tests that more often than not we have to be careful not to miss them. I have been embarrassed by missing vitamin C on more than one occasion.

These vitamins are also checked after gastric band surgery for a few years. Specialists like to test for everything, so once in a while I would see patients come in with these tests where I must be meticulous. I offer more water, as there are many tubes that we must take to ensure we have everything and draining a patient dehydrates them. After several years, not as many tests are requested by the specialist and the patient can then see their doctor for a general checkup.

The man with the metanephrines blood test

Once in a while, a patient will come in with a blood test that involves an enormous amount of work to check the adrenal glands. In medical centres, phlebotomists typically ask for a bed in the nurse's treatment room so the collection centre room can be free for other patients. In other centres, there can be more than one room, with another room to be used for other patients.

A patient needs to lie down for half an hour and be as relaxed as possible. Also, the patient needs to be fasting, and only drink water.

For this story, a patient had just seen their doctor. At one stage, this doctor decided to add the metanephrines blood test for nearly every patient that came by. The patient gave me the form that the doctor had given him, and I asked him if he could lie down for half an hour and if he had fasted.

The doctor then realised some of the prerequisites for the test, and a lightbulb went on in his mind. He asked 'lie down for half an hour?' and I said 'yes'. He then took the form off me and put a line through that test. He then refrained from adding that test onto patients' forms from then on, unless it was absolutely necessary.

The woman with metanephrines

On a Saturday morning, a woman came into a recent collection centre with a metanephrines blood test. As it was a Saturday, she had enough time to spare for the unusual test. I then got her to lie down in another room which had a bed and put the timer on for half an hour. I then saw to the other patients in the waiting room until the half hour was nearly up.

These tests are easy to complete for the patient, but from our end are complicated. After we take the blood test, labelling is the easiest of the procedures. Then, we need to put the tube for this test into the centrifuge for 10 minutes. After this, we separate the plasma at the top of the tubes into a separate tube. We then freeze the separated tubes overnight.

I showed the patient what needed to happen to the blood test afterwards, and she was very surprised. She thought it was an easy 5 minute test after lying down for 30 minutes.

The woman who needed the ACTH and cortisol levels checked

It was an afternoon shift shortly before closing on a Friday. A woman came into the collection centre and handed me the form. It was one of those tests which would have taken quite some time to prepare, and I would have had to have worked overtime to ensure everything was properly done.

One of those tests was for an afternoon cortisol. The problem was that it was way past the time that the doctor wanted for the cortisol, and I did explain that to the patient but could go ahead because that was procedure. Another was for the ACTH test, which has always been complicated to prepare. There would have been quite an amount of overtime if I had completed the test at the time.

The patient told me that she had to wait for her husband to come home to look after her children. As every collection centre is child friendly, I advised her of that and suggested she took her children with her. For her, it would have been around 5 minutes to complete the test, and many children have waited for their parent to have a blood test. However, she didn't want to do that so waited for her husband and by the time he had arrived, it was already very close to closing time. I suggested other centres that were open longer, but she refused.

For the ACTH test, the tubes are refrigerated. We need to obtain 2 tubes from the fridge, and then not mix them up with any other similar tubes for any other tests. After we take the specimen, we then put the these particular tubes into the centrifuge for 10 minutes. We then separate the plasma from these tubes, which are actually quite small in size, into a separate tube. We put the tubes into a freezer overnight.

There was a lot involved. I advised the patient what the procedure was, and she told me she'd come back another time.

The next week, she came back into the centre. By this time, her form was probably scrunched into a ball because it took a while to unfold it. She had come in not even half an hour until closing time. I completed the test for her and followed all procedures. I still had to claim overtime, because she still had come too soon to closing time for me to be able to close on time.

Chapter 11 - Other tests that need to be frozen

There are several other tests that need to go into the freezer overnight. These have much simpler procedures after the patient has left. Normally, they need to be spun in the centrifuge, and then put into the freezer.

The pregnant woman

A doctor will request many blood tests for a pregnant woman over the whole period of time that she is pregnant. They go through so much during the 9 months. All pregnant women deserve a medal for what their bodies have to go through.

One of the many blood tests a woman has is the first trimester screen (FTS). If they miss that window of time, there's another screen after that, but then the window is closed for that test. There now is another test that a woman can have, and quite a few phlebotomists have confused the two. I'm one of them. At the time, the other test was so new we hadn't been given training on it until after a certain period of time. Mistakes do happen as we are human.

A while ago, a woman walked into a daytime collection centre needing an FTS. She had no idea what it was, or what it tested. The doctor had written FTS on the form. She thought I would know, so asked me what the difference was in having an FTS rather than a genetic carrier screen (GCS).

As I have never been been able to have children, I was at a loss what it all meant. I then tried to contact a number of people to help me understand what it meant so I could explain it to the expectant mother.

The boss who I contacted was a very lovely woman. She knew it well. The FTS tested whether there were chromosome abnormalities with the child. The GCS tested whether there were chromosome abnormalities that could be carried from the mother to the baby, from a genetics viewpoint. This test is on Medicare only once, and if the patient wanted another one they would need to pay a fee. If there were genetic abnormalities, then the prospective father could also be tested.

The patient then went ahead with the FTS, and promised to ask the doctor about the GCS.

The patient with a vitamin B6 test on the form

Recently, there has been new information that the media has become aware of in relation to vitamin B6. Sources became aware that vitamin companies were adding vitamin B6 to all sorts of their supplements. These additions were starting to give people in the wider community an awareness of symptoms of vitamin B6 toxicity. Patients were recently going to their doctors to check their vitamin B6 to see if some of their symptoms could have been from this toxicity.

This is a fasting test, and while I'm doing the blood test I put the tube into my pocket. This is so the specimen is protected from light. After the blood test has been completed, I put a label on the tube, then wrap it in aluminium foil and put another label on the tube so as not to confuse the any wrapped tubes that are already in the freezer. It is then put in the freezer overnight.

A patient and her husband walked into the centre. Both needed a blood test. One needed a general checkup without fasting, and the other assumed that she also could do her test without fasting. However, the form had B6 on it.

She was there because she and her husband had stopped taking vitamin supplements and she in particular wanted to check to see if her levels had decreased, thereby ensuring that she was no longer in the toxic range. I asked her if she wanted to go ahead with everything else or if she no longer wanted to do the test.

She wasn't happy that the doctor hadn't advised that it was a fasting test. I did explain that her doctor wasn't to know due to how many tests our lab had, but she still wasn't happy. I gave her a few choices, but in the end she turned around and said she would do the blood test another time.

The FMBS test (1)

Once in a while, I would see a patient with a form that had a fasting metabolic bone study test (FMBS). This test looks out for osteoporosis, so doctors generally test older patients for this condition. For this test, a patient needs to be fasting and only drink water prior to the test. They also need to be ready with a urine sample that needs to be done as close in time to the blood test as possible.

A patient walked into one of the more recent collection centres that I was in. I then asked if the patient could do their urine sample first. At the same time, I checked to see how easy it would be to do the blood test, and this patient had great veins.

She didn't know if she could do the urine sample. I told her it was non negotiable. The urine sample had to be done first. Not one single phlebotomist would want to be caught out without something in that jar. The patient would have to do the whole test again.

She needed more water, so I gave it to her. She went to the bathroom and I waited… and waited… and another patient came in while I was waiting.

I had to ask the patient in the waiting room to wait a little longer, while wondering if the patient in the bathroom could find any success. She finally did, and came back with a filled urine jar.

This test requires 4 tubes. Two of the tubes needed to be put into the centrifuge straight away, while the other 2 tubes had to wait for a while until being put in the centrifuge. One of the tubes then had to go into the freezer until the next morning.

I disclosed the procedure of the tubes and advised that the results of the test wouldn't be with the doctor until longer due to one of the tubes being in the freezer. The patient was fine with knowing that, and booked a doctor's appointment further into the future for the results of her test.

My FMBS test

Recently, I had an FMBS test. It's actually a bit of a painful test, as one can only drink water. There are a few fasting tests where a black tea or coffee with no sugar would be fine, but this isn't that kind of test.

I have a very weird rare condition which usually isn't found in younger people, so I asked my doctor to do this test to check my bones while I was on annual leave. I went to another centre that opened early to get the test done.

My lovely coworker was inundated! There were quite a few people waiting for her, so I picked a number and then went into the bathroom to obtain a urine specimen.

I had to wait a while longer, and then it was my turn. As I used to have a tendency to faint, I asked to lie down while she did the blood test and everything went well, apart from the one tube of many that she missed. We can all miss a tube, as we are all human.

My coworker hadn't had breakfast at the time, and she looked like she needed a bit of a sugar hit so I gave her a jelly bean. I also had some jelly beans while she finished the blood test. It was great to catch up with her, but I dearly love my breakfast!

Chapter 12 - Nervous patients, and tattoos

Most patients are nervous about blood tests. It's not often that a patient is relaxed about having them. They are a necessary part of life, but one doesn't have to feel joy over them. Once in a while, a patient will watch the whole procedure, although personally I can't watch anything to do with them when the procedure is done on me. I found that some others in the health industry feel a similar way.

I have become more used to nervous patients having blood tests than those that are calm about it. I have told many people they are part of a massive club.

The extremely nervous patient

I am a massive history buff, and sometimes I use my love of history as a method of distraction. This happened recently, so it always gives me a smile when I think about it.

When I walked into work one morning, I had opened up the Boney M song 'Rasputin' on Youtube and had decided to listen to it prior to all patients walking through the door. It had been on the radio earlier, and the song had stuck in my head all morning.

A patient walked into the door with trepidation. She needed a blood test, but hated needles and didn't want to know a single thing that was going on. I ensured all her details were correct, and got ready for the blood test.

By this time, she had gotten her phone out with the intent on trying to distract herself. She told me to distract her by talking about anything. She really needed to take her mind what was going to happen. So I did.

I asked her 'did you know that Queen Catherine the Great of Russia had sex with a horse?'

Just that sentence took her mind off literally everything. She said 'WHAT?' and I said I wasn't sure if it was true or not, but that's what I have read. I then started talking about how interesting history was, and asked if she knew anything about Caligula. By the time that conversation had finished, I had completed the blood test and she hadn't felt a thing.

I then went onto the computer to research to see if Queen Catherine the Great of Russia did in fact have sex with a horse, and found it was very popular myth. It really doesn't matter too much, because I distracted this patient to such an extent that she said it was the best blood test she had ever had.

The man with multiple tattoos

It was during one of my many afternoon shifts, and a man walked in for a blood test. Right from the start, he told me that he was deathly afraid of needles. He wanted the test over and done with as soon as possible. I told him to look away so he didn't have to know what I was doing, and he complied.

I looked at his arms to find a vein, and one arm was completely black from tattoos. There was barely an area on one arm that wasn't covered with tattoos.

Tattoos are easy for phlebotomists because we can pinpoint an area where the vein could be. People assume that having tattoos would be harder rather than easier, but we can focus on a particular area of the tattoo in which to put the needle in and be more successful when there's a tattoo covering the area.

I found a good vein, but he was extremely nervous the whole way through so I asked him how long it usually took to get a tattoo done. He said his blackened arm took several hours. I had to laugh at that. He could handle lying still for several hours while multiple needles went into him, but couldn't handle around 30 seconds for a blood test.

He kept saying 'but it's different'. I'm not entirely sure how, because there's no way on this planet I'll get a tattoo!

The tattooed men terrified of needles

For this story, I was working during the day in a very busy centre. It could have been a Saturday morning. The first patient was a man with several tattoos on his arms. I got everything ready for his blood test, and he started freaking out severely. He kept saying 'get it over with get it over with'.

Of course, it took longer than normal because he hadn't drunk enough water and because he was extremely anxious. I finished the blood test and told him it was all over. He then became very relieved. At all stages of this man's procedure, I made the assumption that he could have been a bikie gang member. He had behaved like a rough and tumble guy who generally looked quite mean.

All paperwork was completed and the patient had left. Another patient came in, of Indian heritage. He was very calm in relation to his blood test.

I then started talking about how bikie gang members are terrified of needles. They come in as if they have something to prove, and lose control at the sight of a small needle. The Indian man couldn't stop laughing. He laughed so hard that he was shaking. It had become a little difficult to complete his blood test because his arm was shaking so hard. I had to ask him to remain still for the rest of the procedure.

Several months later in another centre, another tattooed man walked in with the appearance of being a bikie gang member. He was the first patient in the collection room, and behaved in an extremely nervous manner. He was utterly frightened of the needle, even though he had tattoos all over his arms.

The patient after him was a man of Indian heritage. I seriously felt like it was deja vu. I also made this Indian man laugh with talk about bikie gang members being terrified of needles. The Indian man laughed so hard he was shaking.

It was at this moment that I had to ask if the Indian man had gone to the other centre at any time in the past. He had said no.

The diabetic patient

An older woman came into a more recent centre. She was with her husband, and was already hyperventilating over the blood test as she had a very difficult vein and had had really bad experiences.

I asked her if she had drunk water, and if she wanted to lie down. Her throat was dry from being so nervous so I offered water and she already had a bottle. I asked her to drink up as much as possible. She then laid down on the bed, and became even more nervous. I got everything ready for the test, and then went to her with a blue butterfly needle. I found a very thin vein easily.

By this time, I had used distraction methods for a very long time, and most of the time they worked. For this patient, they definitely worked. As she had an accent, I asked her where she was from and she told me. I then started talking about her country's food, and got her to continue talking throughout the whole procedure.

It took very little time at all, but this patient being distracted helped me finish the procedure with no problems at all. Her husband was really surprised, as he had seen her have some really bad experiences. He told her the procedure was over.

As she was going through a diabetic moment and was feeling the effects of her diabetes, I offered her a jelly bean because her sugars were low. This helped calm her down considerably. As she and her husband were walking out the centre, they couldn't stop thanking me. She told me she will never go anywhere else in the future, and I was her favourite.

The older man

Early on in my career, I was in a really busy centre on a Friday afternoon. A woman came in needing a blood test. It was quite easy to obtain a blood test from her. The centre wasn't busy at the time so we talked for a short while.

She told me her husband had such traumatic memories of blood tests when he was a child that he refused to get a blood test for many years. She had to talk him into getting one and more often than not she was unsuccessful. I told her how I distract nervous patients and she promised to bring him in the next day. She had enormous faith in me.

Unfortunately the next day was an extremely busy Saturday morning. They had to wait quite some time before their number came up. The woman was adamant that her husband wait and used every trick in her book to keep him waiting.

He sat on the chair, becoming more frantic as time went on. I got everything ready and asked for him to look at his wife the whole time. He did that, and then I started distracting him by asking him about his work. He was very enthusiastic while talking about his work, and by the time he had finished talking I had completed the blood test.

I then told him to think and talk about anything and everything else the next time he had his blood test done. Thinking about the blood test itself made him anxious, so talking about something of interest was always going to help bring the anxiety levels down.

Chapter 13 - Differently abled patients

People from all walks of life come into the collection centre. Some come in wheelchairs. Others with walking sticks. Others are also blind. Others have invisible disabilities. We don't discriminate on who comes in, as long as we aren't bullied by the general public and we can do our jobs. Every single person throughout their life has a blood test, no matter who they are or what background they have.

The blind woman

It was during one of my many afternoon shifts, and a woman walked in with a man and a dog. The dog was a service dog, and the centre was not a medical centre so nobody in the vicinity would be able to complain.

I didn't touch the dog, as it was obviously working. The woman said she needed a blood test and handed me the form. It was an easy test. She also had a walking stick.

The man and the dog stayed in the patient's waiting area while I let the woman walk to the chair. She had been there before so she knew the vicinity of where she would be walking.

I had a conversation with her about her dog while I did the blood test, mainly because I love animals. When everything had been completed, I led her back into the waiting room while she gave me permission to pat her dog.

The woman in the wheelchair

It was early afternoon in a very busy centre, and I was relieving one of my coworkers who was away. There was another coworker in this centre, but they were about to leave as their day had finished. A woman in a wheelchair came in with their carer. The room was big enough to fit all of us.

The woman in the wheelchair was very funny. She knew how to tell a joke. Her vein was difficult and I had to take a while to find it. Eventually I did find it, and since there was no pillow I used my very large handbag which I have since replaced. The woman made a hilarious joke about the handbag but it did the job perfectly.

Phlebotomists do blood tests on wheelchair bound patients while they are sitting in the chair. They can't move to the bleeding chair as it would be impossible. We make sure they are comfortable, and then find the vein and do the blood test.

The woman and her carer told me how difficult it was to find a vein and she had had many bruises in her life. I was thankfully successful first go each and every time I saw her.

The very elderly man

I was in a busy centre for a morning shift, and it was towards the end of the shift when a woman walked in with her husband. He was in a wheelchair, and she was pushing him around in the wheelchair. He did not look well.

She showed me the vein to use and told me that arm was the one that was good for phlebotomists for the many blood tests he was having. As there was no bed in this room, I used my very large handbag as a pillow and rested his arm on top of it. I tried that arm, but missed. She then realised it was the other arm, so I tried and was successful with the other arm.

During this time, the patient fell asleep. This woman was *very* worried about her husband. She was behaving very frantically, and begging him to wake up. She kept saying he kept falling asleep all the time. He hadn't uttered a word to me, and I'm wondering if he realised where he was.

Something within me said that he didn't have long to live. This woman loved her husband more than life itself. I'm sure she was devastated at the thought of losing him.

The awesome man in a wheelchair

I was in a daytime collection centre and had been working for a while. At the time, I had a little experience under my belt. More often than not, people who need wheelchairs have this incredible sense of humour. They can bring people to tears of laughter.

A patient wheeled himself into the room and stopped in the centre of the room. This time, I used a pillow as this room had a bed. Of course, I used a butterfly needle to ensure stability of the vein.

Usually, I distract patients using whatever method I think is the best for the patient. This time, the patient was making me laugh so hard I needed to ensure I wasn't about to make a mistake and forget something. I can't remember what he said, but I remember how I felt when he was there.

He was very used to blood tests, as are most differently abled people.

The narcoleptic patient

When I first started working as a phlebotomist, I had 2 wonderful coworkers who were the nicest people one could meet. Neither of them work for the company anymore.

I remember one of the coworkers ask a patient many questions. She was on regular medication to reduce the impact of narcolepsy. The patient was diagnosed a while beforehand, and couldn't work because of it.

This patient was a regular, so we saw her several times while she was being monitored by her doctors. She was very happy to answer any questions, and one of the phlebotomists took great interest in what she had to say. I remember one question was how the patient could drive, and what happened if she was going to fall asleep while driving.

The patient responded with knowing exactly when an attack was going to happen. She would pull over the side of the road and let her body sleep while in the car. When she woke up, she would then carry on with where she was going. This meant that she was approved for driving. She had such full knowledge of her body that she could live a relatively normal life.

Chapter 14 - The health workers

Once in a while, a health worker would come in for a blood test. As they have experience with working in the industry, they feel no fear whatsoever when it comes to blood tests. They are the backbone of making sure the community is healthy, but they need to be looked after as well. While they are the backbone of our communities, they are more often than not a migrant or from First Nation ancestry. Health workers are from all cultures.

The high level nurse

As with everybody, health workers can have either easy to difficult veins. To me, this patient had an easy vein, although she told me not everybody felt that way. I found her vein and while I was doing the blood test, I asked her if she was a nurse. She told me that her profession had been in a more managerial capacity.

She told me her level of responsibility. I had the utmost respect for her. She explained that she no longer saw patients and she also taught at a university.

The social worker

In a more recent centre, a woman came into the collection centre needing a blood test. She had a very easy vein. She was also very calm and collected.

As usual, while I was doing the blood test I started having a conversation with her. She was very easy to talk with. My question for her was if she was a nurse. She then asked me 'why does everyone think I'm a nurse? You're not the first person who has said that'. I told her that it was her demeanour. Every part of her behaved as if she was a nurse.

She actually did study to be a nurse and did some work, but found that it wasn't for her. She much preferred to be in social work where she could help people within the community. I then asked her if she'd ever go back to nursing, and she said no. She loved being in the community too much.

The doctor with the wriggliest vein ever

I had had a couple of years experience when a doctor came into a centre needing a general blood test. He knew his body extremely well. He had the biggest vein I had ever seen, and I thought to myself 'this will be easy'.

The doctor then warned me that while the vein was extremely large, it also moved around. He had had really painful experiences with phlebotomists and other doctors overestimating themselves. I felt the vein, and he was right. The vein moved around like it was dancing.

I started using a trick a previous mentor had taught me. The vein moved around under my fingers. It was also very hard to the touch. I had never felt a vein quite like it.

While I did get the vein first go, it was a difficult bleed. It took a lot of skill to keep that vein still enough to accept a needle. The doctor certainly knew what he was talking about!

Chapter 15 - Glucose tolerance tests

Glucose tolerance tests (GTT) are known as one of the most frustrating tests out of all the tests phlebotomists do. This is a 2 hour test and is fasting with the patient only drinking water beforehand. Patients need to have 3 blood tests in total. The first is a fasting blood test, and then the patient drinks a bottle of glucose from which I have been advised tastes like flat lemonade. Pregnant women aren't the only patients that do this test. It's to check to see if a patient is going to be diagnosed with diabetes.

These stories are going to focus on patients who aren't pregnant, yet need to do this test. There are a few.

The man with the one difficult vein in his arm

For a while very early on in my career, I worked in a centre that was close to my home. In many ways it was a bit of a relief. It didn't take long to get home, and my coworkers were awesome.

A man walked into the centre. He told me he was extremely difficult to get any blood from. Others had tried many times and failed. As he worked during the week, he would usually come in on a Saturday morning. For previous blood tests, I had found a vein on the side of his arm that appeared to be his 'old faithful'. I had tried it, and it kept working for me.

Several weeks later, I was rostered at the same centre. He came in and this time he needed the 2 hour GTT. He had more confidence in me than I had at the time. For the first blood test, I tried it and it worked.

For the second blood test after the hour wait, it worked again. Another hour rolls by and by this time I was hoping I'd be third time lucky. Unfortunately, my luck had run out and I had to try again. The poor vein was not happy at being stabbed a third time. I got the vein under control and was able to finish the test.

I then told him that as I moved around a lot, I wasn't going to be rostered at that particular centre for a while. I was probably not going to be at that particular centre ever again. He was disappointed to hear that, as he told me I was one of very few who were successful at obtaining a specimen from him.

The woman who fell asleep

It was quite early on and I was in a centre I enjoyed to go to. An older woman walked into the centre and needed to do the GTT. I explained that she had to be there for 2 hours and as she had done the test before, she was already aware. I then started the procedure and gave her the drink. She then sat down in the waiting room.

Fifteen minutes later, she fell asleep in the chair. I had never seen that before, and have never seen it since. Some patients have said they were tired, but they were usually pregnant women who couldn't sleep during the night because of babies and children and a very full life. Nobody else has fallen asleep shortly after drinking the glucose drink.

Other patients had commented on the woman falling asleep, and the other phlebotomist and I had noticed. We woke her up and asked her if she preferred to lie down on the bed. She said she would, so she settled down and we closed the door to give her privacy.

When she had woken up about half an hour later, she said she had never done that before. She said she knew something was up within her, which is why the doctor had wanted her to do the test. She appeared quite embarrassed.

The other phlebotomist was very experienced in her role. She had never experienced anyone falling asleep straight afterwards either. It was a completely new experience for everyone involved.

After the 2 hours were up, the patient had completed the entirety of the test with no other hiccups, and left to get breakfast.

The man who needed a hand bleed

On a different day and in the same centre as the previous story early on in my career, an older man walked into the centre early in the morning needing a GTT. He had very difficult veins so I suggested getting all the blood tests in his hand which were fabulous for a vampire like me. He agreed.

His veins in his hands were huge. It would have been very difficult to miss.

The first test went like a dream. It was very easy to obtain everything for the first test. He told me it wasn't painful and he would like every single blood test from then on to be done in the hand. I complied.

Once in a while, I convert people to do their test in their hand as it's less painful then trying to dig around for a vein in the arm. This was one of my early converted patients.

All other tests were completed successfully as time went on. Thankfully, there is a television at this centre so he was able to keep entertained while waiting for the entirety of the 2 hours, before going to breakfast.

The older woman who dried up

As I'm not a doctor, I can only assume some results are not going to go in the patient's favour by how the reactions are within the centre. The reactions that patients have after they drink the glucose drink are generally very similar, but once in a while there will be something strange going on.

Recently, an older woman came into the centre needing to have a GTT. She had commented at the time that she didn't know why the doctor wanted her to have the test, but she knew she had to stay for the 2 hours.

When a patient comes in for a GTT, it's during the fasting period so I get the patient settled while other patients are waiting for their blood tests. It takes several minutes only, and then I can organise myself for everyone else while the patient waits for the hour to tick by in the waiting room.

This is what happens initially, but by the time the 2 hours are nearly up I am able to have conversations with the patient to waste a little of their time and only if they wish to break their boredom.

I had some lovely conversations with this patient. She was very talkative. I'm from an Irish heritage, so it suited me.

She told me throughout the whole time that she had drunk water in the morning but she was *very* thirsty throughout the entirety of the 2 hours. This was a bit of a warning sign for me. Patients can drink water before the test, but we do limit the amount of a water a patient has so the sugars aren't diluted too much throughout the procedure and the results are more accurate.

She said that she has started to drink a lot of water and she was always thirsty. She was desperate for water. She told her doctor that, which was why the doctor wanted her to do this test. It appeared that the doctor was insistent on her having the test and was very concerned.

The first and second tests were fine. I was able to collect the necessary specimens. The woman also needed to do a urine test. She had gone prior to walking into the centre, but had 2 hours to try to do one. For the entirety of the time, she felt unable to go, even after drinking the large glucose drink. That was another warning sign for me. Most patients have no trouble doing their urine sample in between the 2 hour time limit.

The third test was extremely difficult. She was completely dehydrated. There was nothing left in her. I had to give her some water just to enable me to obtain some kind of sample from her.

This was really unusual. While she walked out the door hoping that she wouldn't be diagnosed with diabetes, I'm sure the results would give the doctor indication that something strange was up. Her reactions to the blood tests didn't show the norm for what happens during the GTT at all. I told her I hoped so too, even though in my mind I wondered if she was soon going to be diagnosed with diabetes. As I am not a doctor, I wasn't going to say anything that could concern her as it wasn't my place.

These are circumstances where we need to check the psychology of the situation. I had written that the final test was difficult on the form, so the lab would be aware.

The extremely difficult man

There is a geographical area where very few people drink water. It's an area that is a little frustrating for all the phlebotomists who work in that area. Sometimes, we need all the help we can get. No matter how many times we beg patients to drink water, it just doesn't happen. Patients would tell us that they didn't like the taste of water. I would be very confused, as I believe water tastes refreshing and there's no actual real taste to it. It's the actual elixir of life.

This story is from one of those collection centres, and next to nobody had drunk water on this day. It was a Saturday morning. The patient had to wait a while because in this centre, there was a doctor who kept checking nearly every single patient for more tests than can be imagined. I had 5 patients previously with all the same time consuming tests.

This patient was quite grumpy as he had to fast. I had asked him if he had fasted, and he said yes. I then asked if he had drunk any water. He said he couldn't stand to drink water so of course he hadn't. He was there for a GTT.

I explained to him that it was a 2 hour test and begged him to drink some water beforehand to ensure it went easier for him. He kept refusing. I couldn't force him to drink water, so started the test.

He told me he hated blood tests because they were really painful for him. I told him it was because he didn't drink water. I guess he probably didn't believe me. All of his blood tests were painful for him, but the last one was the most painful.

After a while, by the time the third blood test of a GTT is completed the body can become very sensitive. A patient has had nothing but of bottle of glucose for quite some time, and right at the end many patients have told me that the third blood test is the most painful of all of them. This is no matter how ready a patient feels.

If a patient hasn't drunk any water beforehand and refuses to drink it, then it becomes even more painful. This patient didn't understand that his body was screaming out for water, but he was determined not to drink it. He told me it was the most painful blood test he had ever had.

Chapter 16 - Helicobacter breath tests

Helicobacter breath tests are unusual tests that have a timer for 10 minutes. There are quite a few requirements before a patient can do this test to ensure a proper result can be found. This is the only test where fasting means not a drop of anything can touch the mouth for a period of between 4 and 6 hours. If someone goes without for longer, I complete the test to get it out of the way for the patient.

Patients also need to wait for 30 days or more after finishing antibiotics. There are specific requirements in relation to certain stomach medications. This is to ensure the result is as accurate as possible. Helicobacter tests check for a certain bacteria within the stomach. If this bacteria isn't killed with antibiotics, then it can eat outside of the stomach and cause severe problems. It can also cause death. The breath test is the most precise way of finding the bacteria.

The patient takes a tablet that has granules in it that attach to the bacteria. It is only then that the patient can have some water. Three minutes need to go by before the patient is given some more water. After 7 minutes, the patient is then told to take a deep breath and hold. At the go ahead, the patient blows hard into a ballon. The test is then over and the patient can then leave.

This bacteria was actually found by a Perth scientist who wasn't initially believed by the scientific community. He had found a way to find the bacteria, along with a cure for it. He drank the bacteria to make himself sick, then used the cure and recorded all the results. For this, he won a Nobel prize.

These are some of the more unusual stories of some patients who come into collection centres to have this test.

The man who took a deep breath and didn't close his mouth

This was near the start of my career, and I was in a centre close to home on a Saturday morning. I was with a lovely coworker. It was nearly at the end of the shift, and we were cleaning up as per our requirements.

The patient walked in with a breath test on his request form. There was enough time, so I brought him into my collection room. By this time, all other patients had left so he was the only one there. He took the tablet and water, and I did all the paperwork in the meantime. We then waited for the timer to buzz for the next steps.

Right at the end, I tell the patient to take a deep breath and hold. I had assumed that everyone knew how to take a deep breath and hold. The mouth closes so that the breath can stay within the lungs. With this patient, I was very wrong. He left his mouth open for some reason. I was very perplexed.

At that time, we had to wear masks. I felt it beneficial to take my mask off to show him what I meant by taking a deep breath and holding it. So I showed him, and he did it but as soon as I started breathing again, so did he.

It was at this time that I asked my coworker for help. My coworker told me that I was scaring him, so she tried. She got about as far as I did with this patient. She kept asking him to take the deep breath, and he'd take a deep breath and then breathe out straight away.

She then decided that the next time he took a deep breath, she would tell him to blow into the balloon anyway. She said that he would have failed this test, but we were going absolutely nowhere with him and we needed to have at least something. He would probably have needed to do the test again another time.

This took all the time we had before the centre closed, so we let him on his way for the rest of his day. By that time, we were both still shaking our heads wondering how it all happened.

The woman who refused the tablet

I was in a centre that had become busy at the time, although in general this centre wasn't typically that busy. I was a relief moving around as the usual phlebotomist was on annual leave. It was a small centre in a medical centre, so the waiting room was busy with patients for blood tests as well as patients waiting for doctors. We usually only know if someone is for us by the number the patient is holding in their hands.

A woman came into the centre for a blood test. She had stomach problems at the time so the doctor wanted to know the results of quite a few tests. One of the tests was for the breath test.

I gave her all the details about the test, and told her that she'd have to come back to complete the breath test as she had other blood tests and had drunk water beforehand. She said she was fine about it, but hated blood tests so had hoped that would be the end of that part of the procedure. I then gave her paperwork so she could come back.

A day or so later, she came back for the breath test. I then got out the box with all the equipment to start the test. The patient then noticed that there was a tablet.

She had dreadlocks. I should have known there would be something different about her. She asked me what was in the tablet and I said the usual of what I tell everyone - it has a very slight amount of Carbon 13 in it, and in about 1000 years her ancestors may or may not be able to find her. Since Carbon 13 is in nearly everything including us, I thought nothing about it. It was a way of trying to lighten the mood.

She then told me that she was refusing the tablet because 'it wasn't natural' and she only put natural products into her body. She just kept saying it wasn't natural, so she wasn't having it.

I was a bit surprised by her reaction, but there's not much I could have done about it. I told her it was the most precise test to find the bacteria that may have been in her body, but there is a blood test as well but that test is nowhere near as precise as the breath test. She said she didn't want to have another blood test as she hated them.

I then tried to find a way for the blood test for helicobacter to be added onto the tests that I had already completed the day or so beforehand. The reception staff were really lovely, and helped me find a doctor to add the test on. I then made a phone call to the lab and sent over the paperwork.

While I had been ultimately successful with this patient from a generic point of view, I still felt that I had to explain to one of my bosses what had happened. I was quite frustrated by the experience.

The patient who popped the balloon

As it is quite hard to blow into the balloon, I have advised people to blow as if it's a party balloon. Just like a party balloon, there's a barrier that one has to blow past in order to start blowing the balloon up. For many people, this can be quite difficult. Many have had to use more than one breath to see any kind of success.

A man walked into a more recent collection centre. His form stated that he needed to have the breath test done. I explained what was going to happen for each step of the way. He was fine with taking the tablet and water, so I started the timer.

I explained to the man that it's like a party balloon and to blow hard when the time comes. All paperwork was sorted, and the time on the timer runs nearly to the end so I get him to take a deep breath for the last 10 or so seconds as per requirements.

As soon as the time was up and he was ready to blow, the patient had his breath ready… and blew so hard that I heard a pop.

This was the first time I had ever heard the balloon pop like it did. I was surprised at his lungs! I then asked 'did you just pop it?' and he said it sounded like it but to send it through. He thought it could have been fine, but I asked him to blow into another balloon just in case and I threw the original one in the bin.

I got the second balloon prepared and he blew not as strongly into it. We then looked into the bin to check the original and it had already started deflating, so he had definitely popped the balloon.

A short while later, he came into the collection room again. Due to the experiences of the first test, the results were inconclusive so the doctor asked him to do the test again. He made a promise to never blow so hard into the balloon again.

I now make a concerted effort to advise patients to think of it as a party balloon, but to never blow so hard as to pop it. I once said that to another patient shortly before they had to blow into the balloon and they nearly couldn't hold their laughter in time to blow into the balloon.

It was definitely a lesson learned to check each patient's lung capacity before asking them to blow hard into a balloon.

Chapter 17 - Drug and alcohol tests

There are only a few centres that are open for these tests. Quite a few patients walk in expecting to be able to do these tests anywhere, when in fact they can't because not every centre has the paperwork or facilities to do them. There are a few reasons why a patient would need to have drug and alcohol tests. There are standards and a chain of custody involved and not every centre has the chain of custody forms.

With all of these tests, patients need to limit how much water they drink. If they drink too much, then their urine is too clear and no results can be found by the lab. The urine has to be yellow in colour. Otherwise, the specimen is rejected and the patient has to complete the test again.

Most of the time, the reasons are for commercial use. When patients go into the mines for work, they need to be lucid at all times because the work is dangerous. Certain drugs and alcohol can reduce the lucidity of patients, so organisations ensure that patients will be able to complete their work without any influences or negative interactions.

Doctors can also request for drug and alcohol tests for ADHD medications. Usually, this is to test the baseline shortly before the patient is given medication. These tests are on Medicare. The procedure is complicated. Some patients are required to have a chain of custody, and some just need to give us a full urine jar. It's up to the doctor and whether they wish to write the standards on the form. If the form doesn't have any standards on it, then any centre can do it in accordance with procedures.

Another reason why drug and alcohol is requested is for legal reasons. Courts can demand that certain needs are met before a parent can see their child, as one example. This includes not being under the influence of certain drugs. It's up to the the relevant departments to advise in relation to this aspect, and I haven't seen many of these patients in my working life.

These are a few stories about what has happened in relation to this test.

The woman who just couldn't

I was at a centre for several days a while ago which had a drug and alcohol facility. In most centres that are used for drug and alcohol, there are cameras and a monitor outside that doesn't record. In this centre, there were no cameras and phlebotomists had to stand within the vicinity of the toilet area to ensure all standards were met for supervised drug and alcohol tests.

A woman walked into the centre needing to have a drug and alcohol test done. It needed to be supervised, so I advised that I had to stay in the room. She was fine with that.

I completed all the paperwork and then we walk into the room. She went into the toilet area with the jar, and… nothing. She had the worst stage fright I had ever seen. She said she couldn't do it, but it had to be done that day and that was that. She asked for more time and I advised her to start walking around the carpark area. I also advised at the time that she had to limit how much water she had to drink.

So she started walking around the carpark. This was near the middle of the day, so she had time. Other patients came and went, and she was still walking around the carpark. Once in a while, she would come in and try again. She still had stage fright, so started walking around the carpark again.

Other coworkers had started commenting about the patient who was determined to do her drug and alcohol test, but still had the worst stage fright they had ever seen. I told the coworkers that she was determined to do it but each time she went in, all of a sudden she froze up and couldn't do it.

She kept telling me she was desperate to go each and every time. Around 3 hours later, it was close to closing time and I had to tell her that she needed to do it, or come back another time. She finally went in for a last time, and the stage fright left her. She got it done, although the urine was bordering slightly on the clear side.

Her creatinine levels only just made it, and she was finally able to go home. It was the longest time that I had ever seen a patient so determined, yet so unable. When I finally sent the specimen to my coworkers, they exclaimed that they couldn't believe how much patience I had for this one woman. They were even more surprised that I got a sample to give them.

The man who took way too much

I had been working as a relief for a while when this patient came in for his usual drug and alcohol test and saw one of my newer coworkers. I told her that I was there if she needed me, but as her door was open and I could hear her, I knew she was struggling with this patient.

This man was very rude and abrasive. He appeared quite violent and threatening. He disclosed so many medications that it took a really long time to write everything down. My coworker kept asking him to spell his medications, and he started abusing her.

He also had 2 forms and requested if the same urine could be done for both forms. I said yes, because to say no would have put both me and my coworker in an untenable situation. I started writing on both forms, and then got him to do his sample. He couldn't quite fill the jar to the appropriate level that was needed. He then asked if that was enough, and I had to say yes to that.

As it was, both forms had to be completed separately with 2 different samples. Only one form was accepted. It was actually a breach of procedure to try to put 2 companies with the same sample, but my coworker and I both felt threatened by this patient.

A few days later, I was in the same room and this patient walked in again. He asked why one company got results and the other company hadn't. I contacted the lab and asked them why. They told me that the procedure was breached so they picked one company. They asked me why I did it and I told them how abusive and abrasive this patient was, and saying yes to him got us away from the threat of him. They understood, but still couldn't change procedure.

As it turned out, he was listening at the doorway instead of waiting in the waiting room like I had asked. He overheard me telling the lab how violent he was. He had disappeared by the time I finished the phone call.

A few weeks after, I was at that centre again and I spoke to an experienced coworker about this patient. She told me that a few times she had told him to leave the centre without completing his test because he had become far too violent and abusive for her to complete the test. She said he was on so many uppers and downers she was surprised that he was accepted for work.

The man who did something dodgy

The one thing we were told during our phlebotomy course at TAFE was that we had to act normal during drug and alcohol tests even if something dodgy was going on. We had to keep going, and make the patient assume that everything was successful. Most of the time, people who do drug and alcohol tests know not to even bother to try. Once in a while a patient will assume that they got away with something.

I was in a drug and alcohol centre when a man walked into the centre. It was for a supervised test. At the time, I didn't think to get him to take his jacket off as it was cold and I could see everything that was going on. He also checked his pockets in his jacket in front of me and claimed there was nothing in them. I knew when someone had successfully performed their duty of urinating into the jar because I had the monitor on outside the bathroom.

He taken all his belongings out of his pockets and placed them on the table in the collection room. I made him wash his hands and dry them in front of me. He then went into the toilet area, and slowly backed away from the camera into a blind spot.

At no stage did he go anywhere near the toilet. All of a sudden, there was a full jar of urine! The patient must have assumed that I was dumb to not recognise what was going on. He obviously had the urine in one of the pockets of his jacket or elsewhere on his body.

I knew exactly what he had done. At all times, however, I let him assume that he had gotten away with it. I wrote everything in accordance with the chain of custody form. I filled out all details as if he was successful. I let him sign and initial everything. I then let him go on his way, making him at all times assume that I hadn't seen everything he did.

As soon as he left, I then wrote what had happened on the chain of custody form. I wasn't going to let him get away with possibly hurting his coworkers on site. There was no knowledge of what he had taken and how bad or good it was. As he was trying to keep it a secret, he definitely had something to hide.

I'm sure he was rejected for his next trip to the site. I hope he realised that it was for not just his wellbeing, but the wellbeing of his coworkers that I did this.

The man who did something really dodgy

For us, it's a job to do everything properly, including the supervision of the urine going into the jar. For that component of the job, we see far too many genitals to get excited about it. It's not the most fun job. For some companies, they pay drug and alcohol collectors very large amounts of money because of the potential danger involved.

I was in an extremely busy centre and on my own when this patient walked in and waited for his turn to come. He was with his girlfriend, and they waited very patiently. I finally got to him, and he said he wanted to pay for his own drug and alcohol test. He said there was something weird about the company doing it, so he wanted to confirm that he would pass the test. He had told me that he was around a person who was smoking marijuana, but he didn't smoke any himself but it showed up because of the other person.

I didn't know exactly what had happened beforehand, but started the procedure and supervised his specimen. I then checked it, and it came back clear, although the creatinine levels were borderline. I checked that component with an eagle eye as it was very close to failing. To me, it appeared that his specimen had passed. I did everything as per protocol, and sent the results to the lab.

After about an hour, the lab contacted me. They told me the story about this particular patient. He was in another centre far away and did his test according to company procedure with the company he worked at. He failed the test. They found marijuana in his system. So he drove all the way to another place, and drank a lot of water in the meantime. He then took the test with me, and passed.

The company was absolutely furious. They questioned the ability of the lab to do the job properly, even though this patient was determined to be very dodgy. They demanded answers on how this could have happened.

Thankfully, I kept the jar for that patient, along with all other jars. The lab asked me for the jar, and I gave it to them. They then told me that I should have failed the creatinine, but it's the eye of the phlebotomist that determines whether it passes or not. It can be difficult to determine when the colour and the creatinine are borderline.

The lab tested the specimen, and found that the patient had lied to me about how much was in his system. He was smoking it on a regular basis. He failed and lost his job. All because he lied.

The man with clear urine

It was one of those days when I was at a centre for which I had to supervise in the bathroom. There were no cameras so for supervised tests I had to be in the room. It was on a Saturday and towards the end of the shift.

A patient came in for a drug and alcohol test. I wrote all of the details on the form and then took him into the room. He initially had difficulty to start, but then everything went as usual and a specimen was obtained. I checked the temperature and it was as expected. I then checked the creatinine levels, having noticed his urine looked *very* clear. It nearly looked like water.

Unfortunately for this poor fellow, the creatinine level looked like it had failed. I told him I could send everything to the lab, but he would probably have to do the test again. He told me that he kept failing the test all the time because he had severe stage fright. I told him I understood, and it might have been better if he went to another centre where there were cameras instead.

He told me he would try his luck another day, and he walked out of the centre without the specimen reaching the lab.

The man who just couldn't

This was a while ago, and I was in a very supportive centre. A man came into the centre for a drug and alcohol test. He told me that he didn't let anyone watch him urinate - not even his family members. All of his paperwork stated that he had to be supervised.

At the time, I remember asking him if he could do it. He said he was going to try. I started the procedure and took him to the bathroom. There were cameras in this centre, and a monitor for me to watch. He went in, and then got horrible stage fright. He took all his clothes off. He tried to get comfortable. It just wasn't going to happen.

He then put his clothes back on and started verbally abusing me. I waited until he had finished, and then a coworker said if he contacted his boss and asked for an indirect supervision we could write it on the form. Then, we wouldn't have to watch and he could complete the test.

We went back into the room and he contacted his boss. I spoke to his boss and told him the situation and asked for his approval to complete the test as unsupervised. Thankfully, the patient's boss said yes, and he was able to complete the test. I asked the boss to write unsupervised for every drug and alcohol test this patient would have in the future, and the boss agreed.

Afterwards, he apologised profusely. He hadn't meant to treat me so horribly. I told him I understood and said goodbye to him as he went to enjoy the rest of his day.

Chapter 18 - The bosses

I have had a few really humorous experiences with some of my bosses, so thought I'd write some of these stories in. As phlebotomists deal with people in the community all the time, we need support from managers at all levels. These stories show the greatest level of support.

The donuts

I had worked for several months for the company, and was a relief going everywhere at this point in time. I had been rostered on a Friday and Saturday in the same centre, although sometimes my shift moved early the next morning and I was placed somewhere else.

I had requested from one boss on the Friday morning if I was going to remain at the centre the next day because I wanted to buy donuts for lunch as a dessert and leave any remaining donuts in the fridge at the collection centre. The centre was extremely busy and I wanted to reward myself. I wanted to eat the remaining donut on the Saturday after that very busy shift.

At the time, I also wished to do further study. I had completed one subject of another TAFE course, and wanted to complete more so wanted to give a heads up to my immediate bosses about it. As the company needed me at all times, they requested for me to put off my further study for a while into the future.

After a short while, I realised during the conversation about my studies that this boss had me on speaker. In the middle of the conversation, for which I agreed to forgo on extra studies, another boss told me that after my Friday shift they were all going to go to the centre and take all my donuts from the fridge and eat them.

All they heard on the other end of the phone was me saying 'no no no no no'. They laughed really loud and long over that. They thought I was hilarious.

The next day, I wasn't moved from the centre so I opened the fridge to see if my donut was still there. It was, and it tasted really good after my shift ended.

For quite some time afterwards, one of my bosses kept teasing and laughing about my love for donut. In another centre at a later period of time, she gave me a donut for me to make up for teasing me about donuts. I didn't care, because I got more donuts.

The heat temperature labels

I am good with computer programs, but if there's something physically slightly technical or finicky, I'm absolutely hopeless. This is what happened one time with the machine we used to print out labels.

In one of the centres, I had to replace the labels in the label machine. It was probably the first or second time I had done it, so this was a while ago. I put the labels into the machine and then clicked print to print out a label. It was blank. I thought I had done everything to fix it, and that it needed ink, so I called my boss.

I asked my boss for more ink for the label machine. She then couldn't stop laughing. I had to wait until she finished before she told me there was no ink and it was heat generated. I must not have put the labels in properly.

I checked the machine again, and curled the labels under a little nook area. Then I clicked to print again. It finally worked.

There's a few times I have made this boss laugh, but I doubt I made her laugh as heartily as this time.

The hope for winning lotto

A while ago, I was given a room during the day for a while. My roster was a bit crazy, so this was only for a few months until a less crazy roster was given to me.

A more recent boss walked into the room to see how I was going. She asked me how I liked the room and if I was comfortable in it. I was deadpan when I told her that I was only working while waiting until I had won lotto.

She looked at me quite shocked. She spluttered with her words for a few seconds, then told me to think of her when I had won. For a while, she told me to remember her for when I won lotto each time she came to visit me. It's a bit of a hilarious story, because I probably looked so serious about winning lotto that my boss believed that one day I would win.

After that, I have said to some coworkers at the lab and patients whether I had won lotto or not. To date, I definitely haven't won anything.

Chapter 19 - The LGBTQIA+ community

There are many reasons why we would be seeing patients who are from the LGBTQIA+ community. Their health is very important, and they continually get checked to ensure every aspect of their health is looked after by their doctor.

For men who are gay, their sexual health is of utmost importance to them. Quite regularly, they will get all their sexually transmitted diseases (STDs) checked, even if they are in a loving long term relationship. It's normal to see them come in for their routine blood, urine and swab tests. It shows great responsibility.

Trans people get both their sexual health and their hormones regularly checked. They are very brave people, and very vulnerable when they come into a collection centre. I treat them with an enormous amount of care and respect. To me, their gender is who they are and making the decision is probably the hardest and easiest time of their lives.

The easy throat swab

I was in a centre with a bed and it was early in my career. It was afternoon when this particular patient came in, probably after work. The blood test was quite easy. He had great veins and knew exactly what to do.

I then had to do a throat swab. He put his head back and opened his mouth. I saw *exactly* where I should put the swab. There was acceptance of the procedure like nothing

I've ever had before, and nothing I've seen since. I could probably see what he had for lunch!

The procedure went so smoothly, I commented to him on exactly how easy it was to complete it. It was over in seconds, with no fighting and no need for the tongue depressor. He replied 'wonderful! I'll tell my boyfriend that!', and we both laughed.

It was easy to notice that he was gay, and very proud of it. He was a joy to have in the collection room.

The first STD check

This story was while I worked in the afternoons at a very busy centre. I was by myself, and a very nervous young man came into the centre when his number was called. I saw what the doctor had requested, and there were the typical tests required for STDs, as well a urethral swab.

I then explained to this very young man what had to happen in relation to the blood tests and the swab. He was very nervous about needing to do the swab, and I did my utmost to make him feel at ease. I told him that the only men who were used to the swab were much older gay men as they had to do it regularly.

It was while I was doing his blood test that he told me he was gay. I wanted to wrap my arms around him and tell him that he will be alright, in a very motherly way. Due to professionalism, I didn't touch him other than for the blood test, but my motherly instincts came out in full force for a young man I considered very vulnerable about his situation.

I completed all paperwork, and then handed him the swab. I showed him where the bathroom was and told him that if he had any problems, to come back to me and I would help him.

I then brought the next patient in and completed all requirements for that patient. A short while into completing the sample for the next patient, I heard a soft knock on the door. I led the patient out and said goodbye to them. I then looked around, and the young man was sitting on a chair waiting for me.

I led him into the room and I shut the door. I had half expected him to tell me he was successful, but then he told me he dropped it and asked for a new swab. I told him not to worry, and I prepared a new swab as if it was nothing, and threw the old swab he had dropped in his nervousness into the bin.

He told me he now knew what to expect, and wouldn't be dropping the second one. He said it was a surprise with how it felt, but he would get used to it as time went by. His courage gave me even more compassion for him. I knew he would be alright with the choices he had made, even though those choices were very difficult for him at that period of time.

The trans man

Recently, I did a Saturday shift in a room that was shared with another phlebotomist. When it came to a few of the rooms on Saturdays, a number of collectors had complained about how busy it was, so management finally caved in and two phlebotomists were rostered onto Saturday shifts.

This was a total relief. I had worked on a Saturday in this room before, and it was very hectic. At the time and from memory, I had to ask a few patients if they would have liked to have gone elsewhere that didn't have such a wait time.

On this particular Saturday, a woman came in with her teenage son. The woman was very adamant on how her son should be considered. The other phlebotomist and I worked together on all procedures. As I refuse to deadname people and I accept people for who they are, I kept fumbling on whether to call the patient 'he' and 'they'. In the end, the mother laughed as she knew I was trying really hard to make her son feel valued and accepted. I had even typed the son's name onto the labels and ticked the name that the son went by.

Even though it was near the start of the son's journey, the mother was very supportive of her son. Both mother and son were very calm throughout the procedure.

Afterwards, I spoke to the other collector about the situation. I told him that I will always accept whatever name the person would want to go by, rather than what they were born with.

The trans woman just starting out

I was by myself in a room that had been given to me at a later stage in my career. A patient walked in, and as this centre wasn't too busy there was nobody else within the collection centre. I was able to have a really good chat with this patient.

The way this patient looked, plus a number of mannerisms, made me think this person was trans. In a way, I was partially right. They had grown their hair long, and had better looking nails than I could ever have, but then again most people look after their nails infinitely better than I do. They were moving in a more feminine fashion than I could ever do, as well. I had thought at the time - this patient should be a woman.

My biggest concern is that the patient hadn't thought of a new name, so was forced to use their old name. I was forced to write their old name on the labels, as well. I would have loved to have written a new name on the labels for the patient, but at the time I couldn't.

The patient then told me their father refused to believe that they were trans. The father was not supportive, which made this person's life extremely difficult.

As I had a difficult life before working, I found the mountain of compassion this patient needed. While typing into the computer system, however, I didn't find nearly as much compassion from the company as what I wanted, and some of the hormone levels ended up being for 'male' instead of generic. I showed my unhappiness about that, and the patient saw every effort made to accept who they were instead of who others wanted them to be.

At a later time, this patient came in for another blood test. They said because of my acceptance of them who they were, they would only go to me for their blood tests done. By this time, they had picked a very lovely name and had moved. The relief they felt when they could be who they were was palpable. I did tell them that if I won lotto, I wouldn't be working and they were very crestfallen.

The LGBTQIA+ patient

The most ironic thing about starting out is that we sometimes miss before we gain the confidence to be successful. Practice really does make perfect in this job, and the skill necessary needs an enormous amount of confidence. We need to be focused, and have a can do mentality for everyone who comes into the collection centre. We aren't born with it.

A patient came into the centre early on in my career. I was on my own in the afternoon, and they came with their friend. They begged to lie down, and I was in a room that had a bed so I was happy to comply. They then told me that they were deathly afraid of needles, and had a really difficult time with blood tests.

I hadn't gained full confidence in my abilities at the time, and so was probably a little unsure of myself. I went to try to do the blood test, and failed. This patient had only let me try once, as they were terrified.

They told me that there was someone who was able to do their blood test straight away, and while they were trying to find the phlebotomist they thought they'd be able to try their luck and see if they could do it. Unfortunately, at that time they had lucked out with me. These things happen.

They had said they had difficulty trying to find where the other phlebotomist had gone, so I told them exactly where the phlebotomist was and offered for them to see that phlebotomist the next time, so they wouldn't be so terrified the next time.

The trans woman with the very supportive father

The way we get a reputation is whether patients come back to us, or trying to find us when we go elsewhere. A number of phlebotomists have made their mark over time. The collection centre I have recently worked at had a phlebotomist who many people still remember vividly.

A few patients have followed me as well. This trans woman is one of them.

At a previous collection centre, a trans woman with their father walked in. They were very kind people, and a joy to have conversations with. I deliberately changed their labels to include their wanted name, making it apparent on the paperwork who exactly they were.

The trans woman needed to lie down, and I had a bed. I tried to take their mind off what was going on by distracting both the patient and her father with other conversations. By the time they were both distracted, I had successfully completed the blood test.

There was physical disability involving the feet, but the father was so incredibly supportive of his trans daughter. He drove them both to all appointments and took care of his daughter as a proud parent.

When I moved to another centre, it took them a while but they eventually found me. They said because of my compassion of their situation, they only wanted to come to me. Fortunately, I had a bed in that centre as well. It's actually quite an honour to have been found by such nice people

Chapter 20 - The drug users

Every collector will have more than one drug user come into their centre. Most of the time, the veins of drug users have collapsed, making it really difficult to collect much of anything. Every drug user has their own story on how they got to that point, and judging them for their choices is not the best way to have a conversation with them.

I make no judgments on how people live. What I would prefer from drug users is that they are honest with the fact that they use drugs. I like to be given a heads-up on how their veins are. This is all about the professionalism of the job. Life is hard enough without having someone look down their nose at another, so I see every patient as a blank slate with the opportunity to get a sample so their doctor can properly look after them.

More often than not, though, drug users do lie about their drug usage. I am guessing that they are probably ashamed of their drug use. They don't know who I am, and they have highly likely been treated negatively by nearly everyone they have come into contact with.

To me, when they are in the chair, they are just like everyone else.

The woman who hated needles

I was working in a very busy centre on a Saturday and by this time numerous patients had walked in and out of the door, ready for their weekend to start. A young woman came into the centre, and one of the first questions she asked was if she could lie down on the bed.

Of course, I said yes to this. I prepared everything, and then got her to lie down. She looked away, and it was at this time that she told me she was a drug user. Out of immense curiosity, I asked her how she was able to use her drug of choice if she hated needles so much, and she told me she always got a friend to do it for her.

As a distraction method, I started telling her about my story, which had a great many challenges. I told her about the abuse and the domestic violence, and the time when I thought I wouldn't survive any of it. I told her how hard it was to face it, and when I did finally face it to start dealing with it, all I wanted to do was kill myself. I became vulnerable to show her that she wasn't alone.

She then told me her story, which was similar. There was an enormous amount of abuse that she simply couldn't deal with head on. She didn't know where to start, and wondered how to get support to see if she could deal with it.

It was at that time that I told her my first attempt as obtaining the specimen had failed. I had to try again on her other arm, which meant she had to switch to the other side of the bed. She was a bit frantic, but did it anyway. Then we continued on with my distraction method.

She asked me how I was able to deal with everything. I told her that I kept counting every second as it passed. Counting hours or minutes was never going to be enough.

It was too hard and too much could happen, but counting seconds was enough to live in the moment, until the time when I could deal with everything.

I also told her that I wore Lifeline out to such an extent that I was sure everyone at Lifeline knew my voice instantly. I kept asking for help, and along the way I found people who were willing to help. For me, Lifeline was the phone number I needed the most. I then told her the number without looking, as it was still embedded in my memory even after quite a few years.

She thanked me. Not only was I able to collect the specimen the second time, but I gave her information that I hoped would help her along the way in her life.

The guy who lied

For this story, I was in a new centre. It was nice and large, but it didn't have many patients come in as few people knew it was there. The medical centre had only a few doctors. It didn't appear that it would get very busy in the long term, either.

The area was known for its drug users, so it wasn't surprising that this man walked in needing a blood test. It was an urgent test as well, so it was imperative that I collect a sample.

At the time, the policy was that I could try three times to collect a sample. That has since changed. This was early on in my career, and this man was highly likely the first drug user that I had met on a professional basis.

He told me that he used to use, but he had stopped a while ago so wasn't using any longer. I said ok, and then I had a look and I could find very little to go by. I then tried his hand for my second try, and he swore at me and told me that I caused him too much pain in trying to find it. He then said, 'look, I know exactly where to put it so let me put it in'.

This isn't part of policy, but I'm not going to argue with a drug user about where their veins are at. They know which veins hadn't yet collapsed, so I let him put the butterfly needle in and it went in a place that still looked as if it was being used. I got the specimen required.

He wasn't happy with me or my efforts, but I never saw him again. All I know is that he had his own story, and it's not for me to tell.

The guy with one very small vein

I was working in the afternoons in a very busy centre by myself, and at this point in time it was *very* busy. The area was very well known for its drug users, and actually still has quite a reputation. If anyone says they live in this suburb, people from other areas wonder if the person is taking drugs.

A drug user walked in for a test to check some viral loads. This required one very full tube which couldn't be used for any other tests.

I prepared everything, and then went hunting for a vein. It took a *really* long time to even try to go near finding one. The man had admitted he was a drug user, so I knew I was in for a hard time, but I was *very* determined. I finally found a vein in his hand, and put the needle in with success.

The problem with this one little vein is that it went *really* slow. The blood dripped slowly into the tube. The success was a really long one. Finally, I filled the one tube that needed to be full, but the amount of time for the drip of blood was nearly not worth it.

Also, after quite a while the man started complaining that it hurt. I told him that he should have left a better vein for us, because all we wanted to do was make sure the doctors looked after him, and he agreed with that and dealt with the pain.

I then had to put something into 2 more tubes, so the long wait continued. I got at least something in there, but with a very long queue waiting for me I hadn't realised that it had taken half an hour to produce something that I hoped the lab wouldn't reject.

I was finally successful, and wrote 'extremely difficult bleed' on the paperwork. He promised to go back to the hospital the next time as they had the machine which could locate veins, which would make it faster and easier for everyone.

The woman who was very upfront

For this story, I was working the afternoon shift at a very busy centre. It was at around the middle of the shift, and it was starting to become slower in pace. A woman walked into the room for a blood test.

As soon as she sat down, she told me she was a drug user. I was very surprised. Usually, drug users told me they *weren't* using any drugs. She also had great veins, so her admission surprised me even more.

I told her that I didn't care if she took drugs or not, because it wasn't my life. It was her life to deal with everything the way she felt she could. It was not for me to judge her life. I then asked her one thing - to leave her hands for us so the doctors could look after her. She had promised, although I'm not sure if she would have kept that promise down the track. I had just said that the doctors would be looking after her like everyone else, and for us to do our jobs we needed something in order to obtain samples.

Her veins were very easy, and I was able to collect everything I needed with no issues at all.

The woman who was a wrist bleed

I haven't done many wrist bleeds. They are the most difficult, with the most skill required. The vein in the wrist is very thin, and can be extremely difficult to find.

A woman came into the collection centre during one of the very busy late afternoon shifts. Her form required just the usual tests, so I only needed two tubes. Unfortunately, those two tubes ended up being extremely difficult to collect.

As I went through the paperwork, she said 'I don't use'. I thought that was unusual, because I don't ask if someone uses or not. She said she was really difficult. I said ok. She then nearly jumped up in anticipation at the thought of having a blood test. Not one other person in my career has been high with anticipation about having a needle stuck in them. This was another unusual aspect about her.

I then prepared for the blood test, and tried to find a vein on her. I found literally nothing. There was nothing around her arms, and nothing on her hands. I then saw something on her wrist, and decide to get something from that, using a blue butterfly needle.

It was really difficult, but I got a small amount in one tube, with what was in the small tubing of the butterfly into the other tube. She said I could go again in the other wrist if I wanted. She appeared to be really looking forward to needles being put into her. I had said no, and hoped it would be enough after writing 'extremely difficult bleed' on the paperwork.

Shortly after this, it was found that the second tube didn't have what the lab could use for results, so she was asked to come in again. Another phlebotomist tried to collect it, and failed. She had to come back, or go elsewhere.

A month or so later, the same patient had come in yet again for yet another blood test. I hadn't started doing my afternoon shift, but another phlebotomist told me she had failed to find anything. She had asked for one of the most experienced phlebotomists in the state to obtain a sample. That phlebotomist could only obtain the smallest amount in one tube.

I was told by the other phlebotomist who had failed to find anything that this patient had used her wrists to the point of collapse. The patient no longer had even the wrists for us to obtain anything for the lab.

My imagination made me wonder if she wasn't just a user, but also a prostitute who had been abused since she was very young. I hadn't asked about her back story because it wasn't my place. It made me feel very sad for her experiences, and for her life. I still now and again wonder if she's still alive.

The ex drug user

In a more recent collection centre, a man walked in for a blood test. We started going through details, and then I looked at his arm. I found a vein which appeared quite easy. Near it was a bit of a pock mark, which I found curious.

I am the type of person who sometimes asks questions, so I asked the patient what happened to that little area and if they kept giving plasma to the blood banks. With my experience, many people with pock marks around one vein and with many other great veins tend to give plasma and blood.

The patient told me years ago he was a drug user. That was his favourite area to hit, and he hit it hard. He then told me how he got out of using, and it was a really interesting story.

He had some friends he hung out with. Those friends did something that caught the attention of the police. The police found him, and he told the police everything he knew. After this, he wiped all of his friends from his life, got clean, and went in another direction in his life.

He now helps others going through similar situations. The one thing I recognise from his story is that it is very similar to other stories from ex drug users. They turn a corner, sort their lives out, and then are very active in the community helping others. They are the best at helping people in the community due to their experiences.

For this patient, his blood test was very easy. I have also noticed that ex drug users can never look while I'm doing the blood test. It brings back memories for them that they'd rather forget. Considering most of the population can't stand to look while a blood test is being done, I've always been happier when patients are not looking at what I'm doing.

Chapter 21 - The pregnant women

When a woman becomes pregnant, over the course of time there are many blood tests. The first test is the pregnancy test, to see if the levels are increasing. Then comes all the STD and other tests, to check to see if the mother has any issues.

Several weeks later, she can then pay for NIPT tests, and/or have a once in a lifetime only genetics test to see if there are any issues with the chromosomes of the baby or with the parent. About half way through the pregnancy, there can be a GTT, to check whether there's a likelihood for gestational diabetes. A few weeks before birth, the expectant parent is checked for iron, because just like the horror movies the baby is similar to a parasite, sucking the life out of the parent like no tomorrow, while it grows ever so much bigger. It's a total drain on the parent, so iron levels in particular must be checked throughout the whole pregnancy.

All these blood tests were initially unknown to me, as I have never been able to have children. I had undiagnosed endometriosis, and was probably sterile from when I was a teenager. I had accepted my inability to have children very early on, and decided long ago to never have children anyway. My choices are never anyone else's, so whenever someone comes in and are pregnant and wants their child, I am overjoyed for them. If someone decides to have an abortion, I am very supportive for their decision.

Whatever choices another person makes for their life are part of that person's journey which has nothing to do with anyone else. It's not my body, and therefore I have no judgment on anyone else's life or their choices.

The teenager with the grandmother

I was doing the afternoon shift in a very busy centre, and a woman came in with her granddaughter. The woman was quite upset with her granddaughter, and told me why. The granddaughter was in her mid teens, and had fooled around. She was pregnant, and it was very early on in her pregnancy.

The granddaughter was behaving as if she knew everything, and was giving her grandmother looks of exasperation. She was also giving me similar looks, and it was obvious she didn't want to be there and didn't want to hear anymore lectures from her grandmother about her situation.

After some experience of doing this job, one can tell that sometimes teenagers can have the tendency to faint. While I prepared for the blood test with the typical 4 tubes, I asked whether the girl had fainted before. The teenager has the classic response of 'no'. It was one of very few words she wanted to say at that point. The grandmother said yes, she had fainted before and the teenager replied with 'I'll be fine'.

So I started the test with the girl in the chair. After the first 2 tubes, I notice that things weren't going very well for the teenager. Her head started moving from one side to the other in the chair. I quickly stopped the test and told her to lie down on the floor. She thought I was joking, but in a very brusque voice I told her to move it down on the floor RIGHT NOW.

So she quickly got on the floor. I said she would have to do the other tests later, but I wasn't going to finish the blood test at that time because the teenager was about to faint. While she was lying on the floor, I started doing the paperwork so everything not done then could be completed at another time.

The teenager then asked if she could get up, claiming that she felt fine. I took one look at her, and told her to stay there because I wasn't going to have her faint on my watch, especially in such a busy centre when people were waiting.

The grandmother then asked me 'can you please come home with us? I want you to talk like that to my granddaughter all the time! She's actually listening to you'. I said it was part of my job to take care of patients, but inwardly I loved the compliment.

I told the teenager that the next time she had a blood test, she would need to lie down at all times, and that this was just the beginning of all the blood tests she was going to have to have for the duration of the pregnancy. There were many more to come.

The older woman

It was while I was in a recent centre, and a woman in her 40s came in for the STD and other tests, right at the beginning of her pregnancy. We had a very long chat about life, and where it could lead people.

This was her first pregnancy, and she saw no knight in shining armour in her horizon. She had wanted a child with previous ex partners, but nothing came from it. She had worked hard for most of her life, and all she wanted was to have a child.

She had received varied amounts of support for her decision to be a single mother. She was apprehensive about the decision, but quite excited. She had spent thousands of dollars on IVF, and previous efforts had failed. She knew the risks involved due to being a bit older than other mothers, but felt the time was right for her.

I told her some stories about my life to try to help her. Both of my grandmothers were born when their mothers were in their 40s. While both of my grandmothers had other children, there was a very large age difference between them and their siblings. Both of my grandmothers were healthy even though it was the 1920s and medical science was nearly non existent for new mothers.

I had asked about NIPT, and whether she would do this particular test. She said she definitely would, and if there were issues with the chromosomes she would make a decision then. She was not going into having a child closed minded. She felt strong and mature enough to be able to handle whatever life threw at her at that point in time.

The loving new father

For quite some time, I worked nearly every Saturday for more than 2 years. I am assuming that this next story comes from me working on a Saturday. I do remember where I worked - in a very busy centre on my own.

A very nice young couple came in. It appeared that they had just gotten married and were having the family of their dreams. I was very happy for them.

Unfortunately for the new wife, the blood tests requested that she had to fast. Up until that point, she told me she continually felt nausea. In the culture of these prospective parents, fasting meant not drinking any water. I explained to the couple that the machines used for pathology results do accept water so I offered her some. She drank some water, and then I prepared and started the test.

It was by this time that I realised jelly beans could be really helpful for patients to ensure they didn't faint. I finished 2 out of the 4 tubes necessary, and by this time the patient told me she was dizzy. That was the cue that she would soon faint.

As I had finished the tests that required fasting, I turned to her husband quickly and said 'go to my desk and get the jelly beans out. Give her some jelly beans as fast as you can'. The husband did everything I asked very quickly and started feeding his lovely wife some jelly beans.

I was able to finish all samples and she was feeling much better in the chair. Everything was completed as normal after this. The couple was very thankful, and they continued on their way.

The woman who had gastric band surgery

By the time of this story, I was moving around quite a lot, and ended up working in a collection centre attached to a hospital. I had a lot of support, which was an absolute relief for this story.

A pregnant woman walked into the centre for her GTT. She told me that she begged her doctor not to make her do the test. She had been told that anyone who had had gastric band surgery should *never* try to do a GTT, but her doctor was *very* insistent that she do it.

She had come prepared with her own vomit bag. She had many other tests that had to be taken, along with a diabetes test (HBA1C) just in case she couldn't finish the GTT. I got the drink out in preparation, and then proceeded with the fasting test for everything that was on the form. She started drinking from the bottle. About a third of the way through, she started throwing up into the vomit bag.

I am no good when it comes to people vomiting. I have a very difficult time holding my stomach together, even when people (or my cat) start making the sounds that they are about to vomit. I left the room and went to talk to another phlebotomist. I told the other phlebotomist what was going on, and then waited for the vomiting to stop.

When it eventually stopped, I went back into the room and showed her where to discard the vomit bag. I asked her if she was ok and she said yes. She then kept saying 'I told them so I told them so, they should have listened to me'.

Our procedure was that if a patient started vomiting after drinking the bottle of glucose, the test ended and we sent what we had to the lab. That is what I did, and wrote on the GTT form the reason why the test ended so quickly. The patient then left to go about her day.

The lesbian (1)

It was a couple of years into my career, and a woman came into a centre I had never been in before. The room was typical. It wasn't too busy, nor was it quiet.

A woman came in for a pregnancy blood test. I had asked her if she was bleeding, because miscarriage is very common with women in their early pregnancies and we have different procedures that we adhere to when a pregnant woman is bleeding. It becomes urgent, and needs to get to the lab within a certain amount of time.

Unfortunately, it appears that she was bleeding, and she was extremely upset by it. I gave her some time, but she wanted me to get it over and done with.

I told her that she and her partner could try again in the future if she had lost the baby. She then told me that she was a lesbian, and her wife and she had tried before with IVF but it was too expensive to carry on. This was the second time, and they had dearly hoped that this would be it because they had no money left to try again.

I couldn't stop apologising. I felt really awful about my mistake, until there wasn't much more I could say. The only thing I could say was that I would make sure her sample got to the lab as urgently as possible for her.

The lesbian (2)

A woman came in for her initial STD and other tests. I prepared everything, and then make the mistake of assuming (wrongly) that she had a man in her life. She corrected me, and told me that she was in a very loving relationship with her wife and they decided they wanted to have a child.

I was very apologetic. She had told me not to worry, and quite a few people made the mistake. She was very accepting of people's misunderstandings.

I asked her if she had gone to IVF, and she told me there was a particular Facebook group for the LGBTQIA+ community where women could become pregnant without having to go through the expense of IVF. I was very curious, and wanted to advise others in a similar situation how to go about things if they couldn't find the expense.

I asked if I could share this Facebook group with others who wanted to try who were in a similar situation. This woman was very happy for me to do so, as it would mean that I could reach a number of people who would have a better chance to have a family.

The miscarriage

After a couple of years, I had a very unusual roster where I would be working mornings in one centre, then a few afternoons in another centre, as well as every Saturday morning. It was a bit of a gruelling roster, but I accepted it as it gave me some afternoons off.

I was working at an afternoon shift when a woman walked into the centre. She didn't appear happy. I got her in the room, and noticed that she had a pregnancy test on the form, along with the word 'bleeding'.

This was an urgent test. I had to ensure that the lab received the specimen at an appropriate time.

When I looked at the patient, she started crying. She said she was bleeding heavily, and it was obvious she was losing the baby. I gave her time and tissues. She wasn't in the right mind for me to complete any procedures, so time was what she needed to be in a position to handle a blood test.

I was then able to complete the test. She thanked me for giving her that time.

The next day, she walked in for another blood test. I asked her if she was ok, and she said she was. She knew she had had a miscarriage, and the bleeding had nearly stopped. She was much more composed, and had accepted the reality that this wasn't going to be the time when she would be holding a baby in her arms… yet.

The near miscarriage

There's a few stories in relation to near misses, but this one stood out. A patient came in, and I could tell that she wasn't happy. I see on the form that the doctor wanted an urgent blood test for pregnancy.

I asked the patient if she was bleeding. She was. I then started the procedures for urgent blood tests, including checking the time of when the courier would next turn up. It was going to take too long. The courier came at set times during the day, and this specimen ended up needing me to call for a taxi to get the specimen to the lab.

I completed the blood test, and then the patient started crying. I put my hand on her arm to comfort her, then reached for tissues and let her compose herself. I let her cry for as long as she needed. I told her this was going to be urgent, and as soon as she left I would be contacting the taxi for her specimen to go to the lab urgently.

A couple of days later, she came in for another blood test. I asked her how she was, and she told me the baby was fine. She hadn't lost it after all. The levels were increasing and it was a false alarm. I was so happy for her.

The woman who came late

It was in a recent centre, and I had a set time for when to open the centre and when to close it. A woman who was pregnant with her first baby came into the centre shortly before the centre closed. She apologised for being late but wanted me to do one of the many blood tests and she raced to the centre straight after work.

I had done her blood test before, but had forgotten. I couldn't remember her from anyone else. She told me that she only wanted me to do her blood test because of how friendly I was.

For this blood test, I unfortunately missed. I had to try again. I apologised to her, and she told me it was fine and she didn't mind one little bit because I was so friendly and made her feel comfortable. I tried again and was successful with the second time around.

Several weeks later, she came in again shortly before closing time. This time, it was so close to closing time I ended up having to work overtime. She said she couldn't help it, but she really liked the way I did her blood tests. She told me my whole manner helped her make her mind up that I was the only one who she was comfortable with to do her blood tests. It was a wonderful compliment.

The IVF blood tests

There are so many women desperate to have a child. What they have to go through takes courage. The many blood tests, and the many hormones they have to inject, would make a man faint.

I saw one patient recently who was the loveliest woman. If anyone deserved to have everything they wished for, it was this woman. I saw this patient every few days to check her hormone levels. She told me the procedure for it from the IVF clinic.

The first time that she went into the clinic, there was a test run to see how her body would react without hormones being injected. An embryo was embedded when her hormone levels rose to the required level.

Unfortunately, the first time it didn't work. She had lost that embryo. It hadn't implanted into her, so she went back, and the procedure was different.

Every day, she had to inject hormones into her body, and then wait for the blood tests to see when she would be ready to have the embryo imbedded. When her body was finally ready, she needed a very urgent blood test for which I called the taxi. The results needed to be with the doctor within a strict time limit. On that day, I wished her luck for the whole procedure.

A short while later, I saw her again. I was looking at her with anticipation. She looked withdrawn, so I asked her if she had lost the baby again.

She told me it was actually successful. She said as the embryo was a couple of weeks old, she was pregnant for a few weeks. She was reluctant to tell anyone, as she and her husband had been disappointed before, but she had to tell me because I had seen her with her journey.

I was really excited for her, and my hope was that she was finally successful with her first baby, after a really long time waiting.

The abortion (1)

When I first started working, as soon as I saw the pregnancy blood test on a form I would say 'congratulations'. I learned my lesson with a patient who wasn't happy that she was pregnant. She said 'no no no it's not a good time'.

I apologised profusely. The patient had received a lot of judgment from her parents who wanted her to have the child. She had her reasons why she wasn't in a good place to have a child, and she was in two minds about having an abortion.

I told her my story, of how I was unable to have children myself, but that is me and my life. I told her how every person needed to make their decision on their life, and if it wasn't a good time for her then she should make the decision about the direction of her life for herself without anyone telling her what she should do.

I also told her of the abuse I suffered as an unwanted child, and how I would never want that on any child in the world. There are reasons why a woman should make the really hard decision, and it wasn't her parents' choice. She could always have wanted children at a later time when she was ready.

A couple of weeks later, I saw this patient again. She thanked me for the support, and told me she went through with the abortion.

The abortion (2)

I have told my story to a few patients who needed the support necessary to believe in their actions for themselves. In another centre, I saw a patient who had been in a bit of a bad situation. She had become unemployed and her boyfriend had left her, and on top of that she had become pregnant.

It was not the sort of situation where she could envisage having a child. She was very mature about the decision. She knew that children are very hard work. It wasn't that she never wanted to become pregnant. She just didn't want to do it alone and homeless.

She went to the doctor to request for an abortion. Unfortunately, the doctor tried to talk her out of it. He gave information for specialists for pregnancy, as well as blood tests for pregnancy, but this really wasn't what she wanted.

She came to me for the blood tests, and I told her that the blood tests were for pregnancy. She became very confused, and decided to refuse to have the blood tests. So I suggested that she go to a particular women's clinic nearby that could help her with what she wanted for her life. She promised to go there instead.

Shortly afterwards, she came back for a blood test which was much more relevant for what she needed for her life. She thanked me for pointing in the direction where she was listened to by a doctor. I did that blood test for her.

She was very happy to have been given support for what was a very difficult decision.

Chapter 22 - Patients from African background

There are a few reasons why I wanted to separate the stories in relation to different cultures. There are many patients from African background where I live, but also if anyone from other countries read this, then it will hopefully help people understand a few things.

I have been told by some people that people from African backgrounds have thicker skin, or they can't feel pain as much as people from European backgrounds can. Even a patient from an African background once told me their skin was thicker. I hope these stories show that this simply isn't true.

The girl with the very thin vein

I was working in a centre that was open in the mornings in a very quiet centre. A patient walked into the centre needing a blood test. I cannot remember which African country she was from, but she had told me at the time and I was interested in the answer.

She told me that she was very difficult to obtain anything for a blood test, and she wasn't wrong! Her vein was extremely thin. I tried that vein, along with another, and wasn't able to obtain anything. She had to come back a short while later.

When she came back, I tried her vein again and finally got something. Her vein was very thin, and extremely tricky as it moved around quite a lot. I hadn't had the extensive experience that I have now, so it was difficult. It was a very unusual vein in that it was small, thin, and quite obvious but still very difficult.

Her skin wasn't thicker. In fact, her skin was quite thin and the usual for any person her age. Every arm is different, and every vein is different.

The woman with the very easy vein

In a recent centre, a woman came into the centre needing to have her blood test. She was from an African country. More often than not, women from African countries who work in Australia are in the health industry. This woman was a nurse.

She definitely knew her veins. We spoke about the health industry extensively. She was lovely. She showed me her vein, and it was really easy. She actually had 2 very easy veins. On on each arm.

The one thing I noticed about doctors and nurses is that they don't drink nearly enough water. They do advise patients to drink water. I know that, because a doctor having a blood test once told me that they didn't practice what they preached. Doctors and nurses are run off their feet in helping patients so generally don't think about themselves or their own needs.

This nurse hadn't drunk enough water. She was tired, and her job was so intense that she kept forgetting. When I tried to finish the blood test on one arm, it had dried up for the other tube. There was nothing left for that vein, and all because of how dehydrated she was from being run off her feet at her very intense work.

I then tried the other vein and it was successful. It was also less painful for her. She felt the pain from the first try, just like everyone else had when something was not quite right. She didn't feel the pain quite as much with the second try.

The woman with the extremely difficult vein

All veins are different in all people. Some patients have easy veins. Some have difficult veins. As an example, one of my arms looks easy, and the other looks difficult. I spoke to family members, and it appears I got the veins from one arm from my mother and the other from my father. It's actually all genetic.

A woman came into a centre in a flustered manner. She knew she had difficult veins, and there was quite a wait as the centre was very busy at the time. She decided to come back later, because she knew that her veins weren't the best.

She came back when it was much quieter. She was a nurse, and knew exactly how difficult her veins were. She knew I would need extra time to find her vein, and then extract the amount required for the lab to obtain results. She even knew how many tubes I would need.

I checked everywhere, and found something that required a blue butterfly. I then tried my luck, and got this vein first go. It was a relief for both of us that I was successful. This patient knew her body very well, and had more difficulty than could be imagined. She had quite painful experiences, and was previously very bruised. It was quite understandable that she was reluctant.

A short while later, she came in for another blood test. I forget everyone. It's just me. I have a terrible memory for people, just like my grandmother had when she was alive. I couldn't remember this patient, but she definitely remembered me.

She told me that I was successful the first time, so she was going to come to me from then on. I did her blood test, and was successful yet again. She had reminded me where to go, and again it wasn't as painful for her as previous experiences had been.

The man with the very difficult veins

This was a while ago in a very busy centre attached to a medical centre. A patient walked into the centre needing to have a blood test. He was really nice. He was also very tall.

I remember having a great conversation with him. He was very aware that he had very difficult veins. There wasn't a place where he hadn't been poked and prodded in his life. I asked him if he had drunk water, and he hadn't. This made his life much harder.

So I tried, and… nothing. I tried again, and… nothing again.

I really wanted to try again, but at the time the company had procedures that stated I couldn't and he really should have drunk more water. He had felt pain each and every time I tried.

So he had to come back at a later period of time. He had told me that because I was friendly, he wanted me to try again, but luck had it that a coworker got his number and led him into their room. I asked them to see about trying his hand instead of his arm because I had failed in his arm and he was poked too many times. They agreed.

They took him in, and checked his hands. They looked like they had infinitely better veins than his arms. That happens quite a lot. My coworker was successful with obtaining a specimen from him in their room.

After several minutes, he came out of the room and I saw him again. He was very happy with my coworker. From then on, he promised to ask to have blood tests only from his hands. It was far less painful than trying over and over in the arms.

Chapter 23 - Patients from other backgrounds

The reason why I'm writing a story about a First Nations patient in this chapter is because I only have one story that stands out. Many First Nations people are used to painful experiences, so they understand that blood tests can be painful and they don't complain. I try to ensure that blood tests are not painful for anyone, but sometimes they can be a bit painful because it is a medical procedure. First Nations people keep telling me they aren't in any pain, even if they actually are. They are very stoic people who have been through far more than they should have.

Sometimes, I have been the patient while First Nations people have been the health workers who looked after me with incredible competence.

There are so many different cultures in Australia. I relish the thought of trying my skill of remembering to say hello in many different languages. While more often it's the only words I know in the different culture, it goes a long way to connect with a patient. I also try to connect with patients by using food. It's very helpful to be appreciative of the food from different cultures.

The older woman with a history

This was quite some time ago in a very busy centre in the afternoon. At the time, it was quite busy but was slowly dying down. A First Nations Elder came into the centre needing a blood test. It was to check her heart, and it appeared that a doctor was very concerned about her health.

I looked at the form and noticed that it had some urgency to it. I told her it was quite urgent, so I had to ensure the procedure for an urgent blood test was undertaken. I then checked her vein, and she had a really good one in her arm.

I did her blood test, and because the form had stated that she had previous deep vein thrombosis (DVT) on it I asked her if she was on blood thinners. We do have to ask those kinds of questions, because it takes much longer for a patient to hold onto the cotton wool ball before the wound heals.

She told me that she wasn't on anything, nor had she been put on anything to help with the DVTs by any doctor. She told me that she was ignored by the health industry for many years. This horrified me, and showed me that racism still exists within the community today.

Finally, a doctor had listened to her concerns and did something about this Elder's health. I'm sure the patient now has appropriate care. My only thought about this situation is that it took a very long time to help an Elder who should have been helped a long ago in the past.

My story with a great surgeon

Before I commenced studying for the phlebotomy course, I had several health issues which took me into the emergency department (ED). One of those was emergency gallbladder surgery in the middle of Covid lockdown. Another was emergency surgery to remove a 76mm cyst.

My doctor at the time had miscalculated how big it was so thought it was nothing. She then made a phone call to me apologising for miscalculating and told me that if I felt any pain I should go to ED.

A couple of days after the phone call from the doctor, I was in absolute agony so went to ED. I couldn't move. The cyst was very large, and finally decided to cause pain. I don't know why, but it decided to show itself as being there right then and there.

I remember not being able to move, and advising all nursing staff that I wouldn't be able to move without pain. Some of the nurses were telling me it definitely had to be removed, and to make sure I got the surgeon to remove it.

The surgeon then came in and had a conversation with me. He was a First Nations man, and he was very knowledgeable. He refused to remove it, stating that it was a long surgery and he could move me up the list to get it done within the next week. I told him I couldn't move at all and I needed it out as a matter of urgency.

I was able to get the surgery done the next day by another surgeon, but looking back I knew why the First Nations surgeon refused to operate on me. He was an emergency department surgeon. He was there to look after the most extreme cases. If he did my surgery, anyone who needed him would have had to have waited. He couldn't do that to all the other people who needed him more than I did.

For that, I completely understand and respect him even more. I had faith that he would have been a great surgeon. He just wasn't my surgeon at the time.

The short Middle Eastern woman

It was a Saturday morning in a really busy centre. It was a while ago, and this patient still puts a smile on my face. She came from overseas and was with her son. She spoke very little English. Her son lived and worked in Australia and was the translator for her.

They were the first patients to walk in on this very busy Saturday. They came into the room, and the woman tried her utmost to sit on the bleeding chair. It was a bit of a disaster. She was too small for the chair! She had a harder time trying to get onto it than children do.

She was a lovely woman with a great smile. They spoke Arabic and were from the Middle East. By that time, I had many languages up and running on Duolingo and Arabic was one of those languages. I tried my luck with saying the basics to them, like hello and thank you. It made this lovely woman smile even more and look at me with pleasure.

The woman sat on one of the chairs in the room and I got my large handbag out so I could place it under her arm. I did the blood test while she sat on the chair and after completing all details including private health insurance.

The son was very happily surprised that he didn't have to pay anything because of the private health insurance.

Previously, he was told that he had to pay, but that was probably because the private health insurance hadn't been paid for prior to this event. He kept her private health insurance up to date shortly before coming in for a blood test, so it helped him realise that private health insurance for his mother was beneficial.

Several months later, I was at the same centre and the mother and son came in for another blood test for the mother. She recognised me straight away and went to the chair. I actually remembered her, but probably because of her height. She went straight to the chair and put her arm up with the expectation of my bag being placed under her arm.

They were both very happy to see me, and saying shukran was an absolute pleasure to say to them as they were leaving.

The Chinese couple

It was in a really busy centre and I was working as a relief. A Chinese couple came in with their daughter who was translating for them. They both needed blood tests. I went through all details with the daughter for each parent, and then let the first parent sit down. As they couldn't speak much English, all technical aspects in relation to the blood tests had to be run through with the daughter, who spoke in Chinese to ensure everything was considered in accordance with the lab.

The requirements took a while, but the blood tests didn't. In the middle of the blood test for the first parent, I started speaking what little Mandarin that I knew. As they were Mandarin speakers, they were nicely surprised and started laughing in joy. They helped me say all the easiest numbers as I kept forgetting some of them.

They were both relaxed and very happy that I tried to reach out to them with a few words. It made their day that I made an effort. Usually they had their daughter with them to translate while they learned English.

The Afghan woman

In a recent room, a woman with the most beautiful clothes and fashion sense came into the collection room wanting to have a breath test done. She was a lovely woman.

I brought her into the room and found out that she spoke very little English. She was by herself as well. There was no translator available, and no family member. She had come during a time when it wasn't busy. Nobody else was in the centre, so it was a case of trying to understand each other.

As the breath test had quite technical terms attached to it, I opened up google and asked her what her language that she usually spoke was. I did a quick search and found her language in order to translate into her language to make life easier for both of us.

She smiled at that. I was making an effort to bridge gaps. As I touch type, it was easy for me to type down the questions that I needed responses to. She was able to nod or shake her head upon reading the questions in her language, and I was able to then start the test.

Throughout the whole period, I was continually typing questions and explaining what needed to be completed next through the google translation website. The woman understood the words for drinking water in English, although I also used my hands to show her what I meant and she understood that perfectly.

I then also got her take a deep breath at the end of the test, and to hold it to blow the balloon up. As soon as she had blown the balloon up, she was able to go. I was successful with this test because of an online translator.

A few weeks later, the woman came in for a blood test. This time, there were other patients also waiting and it had been quite busy. I had a look at her form and there were a few technical questions that needed to be answered. I had forgotten what her language was, so I had to ask again and she told me.

Again, I opened up an online translator and typed all my questions into the translator. She was able to respond very well. I then did the blood test and ensured all requirements were met. This patient looked very happy that I was trying to find a way to communicate with her in a way that bridged a gap. She was then able to go about her day.

At least one other patient noticed that her English wasn't the best, and he commented to me about that. I breezily stated that I had no problems with communicating with her at all.

I wouldn't have been surprised if she was a refugee, or the mother of a refugee. Afghanistan has an unfortunate history. I'm glad and relieved that this woman lives in Australia, where I could be able to find a way to communicate respectfully with her.

The Korean man

In a recent centre, a man walked in needing to have a blood test. It was a fasting test, and he had complied with the fasting aspect. I asked him some questions in relation to some of the tests, and he hadn't quite understood what I had meant so I changed how I asked the questions.

I had known that he was Korean from the start. He had a Korean name and his facial features were also Korean. He was happily surprised that I noticed. I noticed that his English was actually near perfect. He had a good vein and I was able to easily do his blood test. He then explained about his life.

A few years previously, he owned his own restaurant business. He was then diagnosed with a brain tumour. He went through the surgery and the chemotherapy, and came out the other end but had to relearn many life skills again. It was a really long road that he travelled, but he was finally back to working again.

He had recently started another restaurant business. He had the clothes with his new business on. I started telling him that there's now certain food I couldn't eat because of some of the problems I have with autoimmune conditions.

I loved kimchi, Korean food, Indonesian food and Thai food but as they are based in shellfish I can no longer eat them which makes me sad.

He then told me the good news - he has vegetarian options that don't have shellfish in them. I was very happy to hear that. Unfortunately for me though, I have forgotten the name of his business already or I would have eaten there by now.

The Austrian man

It was a while ago in a small centre attached to a medical centre. An Austrian man walked into the medical centre for an extensive blood test. He didn't have private health insurance, and didn't have Medicare. He was aware that he needed to pay to have the blood tests done.

At the time, the fees surrounding blood tests from my company were different. They changed shortly afterwards. It made our lives as phlebotomists quite frustrating for a while. Not everyone can pay for a blood test, but this man could.

So I checked his veins and they were really good. I confirmed the amount that had to be paid, and straight away the Austrian man paid easily for all of the tests.

He did tell me why he was in Australia at the time, but I forget these types of memories easily. What I do remember was trying to speak German with him. I was quite clumsy, but he was very helpful and he smiled the whole time. He was a really nice man who then went on his way.

The French man

There are certain areas where there are very lovely French restaurants. Unfortunately for me, I haven't been to any of them although I do have intent in the future.

It was early on in my career, and I was working at a large centre with a coworker I got along with very well. I was still moving around a lot as a relief, but for some reason I was put into this centre for a few months. It was midmorning, and a French man came in asking how to go about getting some blood tests. I can't quite recall if he had a form, or if he needed to obtain a form. It was a while ago.

The man had a very thick accent, and I understood him quite well but my coworker was having difficulty. French is the language that I have learned the most. I started talking to this French man in French and we understood each other quite well.

Of course, I tell all French people that I only understand a little of the language so they can speak slower for me, but it's always been a pleasure to speak in another language.

The French man then walked away with the promise of coming back when he had complied with all aspects of the tests he wanted to do.

The Sri Lankan couple

In a recent centre, a Sri Lankan couple came into the centre as the wife needed to have her GTT completed. They were both lovely people, and the husband stayed in the waiting room supporting his wife throughout the whole procedure. I didn't get much time to talk to him until I had cleared the busy room of patients and completed all the administrative duties surrounding all of the patients' paperwork.

I had lovely conversations with the patient while she was in the room. She was very nice and friendly. She then sat down for her last hour, and I got to have a real conversation with her and her husband in the waiting room as all other patients had come and gone by that time.

As they had come from Sri Lanka, they talked about the Tamil people. They told me they considered it unfair that they went through all of the procedures for coming into Australia and had received a visa when other people 'wanted to shortcut the system' and come in as refugees. They said the war in Sri Lanka was horrible for everyone, but the Tamil people should not have received any special treatment.

Our immigration system is known to be quite warped. There are major problems with it, and it all stems from the amount of racism that people show each other. The limitation of acceptance of people drives this horrible system. I am very aware of the faults and flaws of the Australian immigration system, even though I was born here and all sides of my family were born in Australia for generations.

I told this lovely couple my opinion of the immigration system. I told them exactly how racist it is. I said that I believed everyone should be welcome here, and to put restrictions on everyone is a horrible and expensive way to deal with being here. I also said that there is a problem with housing that stems from greedy rich people who want to keep their greed to themselves instead of behaving appropriately for the benefit of the country.

As I have read about the situation involving housing, I placed the blame on the very wealthy and government policy of negative gearing which caters for rich people for the situation that we are in. I told this couple that rich people are buying many properties and leaving them empty for their tax breaks. This therefore is a problem that the government should intervene in, rather than blaming people who want to live in Australia.

The couple understood. They saw everything in a different way, and are hopefully no longer upset with the Tamil people for also wanting to live here, no matter how they arrive in Australia.

The French family

In a recent centre, a woman walked in needing a blood test. She had a French name, so I tried my luck with speaking French with her. I found success, but she wasn't actually from France. Her background was from a French island. I didn't mind, because I figured I could still speak French with her.

She was very accommodating. Her vein was easy, so I had no problems with that. I did have a few issues with understanding her French when she spoke very quickly, and had to ask her to slow down or I started speaking English instead.

It was a very pleasant experience.

Later on, another of her family members needed a blood test. They told me that this particular centre was the one that they all went to, so I had fun with speaking French to them as well.

The Greek man

The most recent centre I have been at has a very multicultural flavour to it. Many people from different background come to this centre for their blood test. It's a joy to try to speak what I can with everyone who comes in.

A man with a Greek background came into the centre. He had lived in Australia for most of his life. His family had come to Australia for a better life, as many Italian and Greek families did several decades ago.

This man still spoke Greek. He was a lovely man who had married a woman from English background. He told me that she had started learning Greek so she understood it quite well.

For me, I once had a Greek boyfriend. That relationship was an extremely horrible experience. The only good thing about that relationship was the food and the fact that I learned some Greek words that I still remember to this day.

I did the man's blood test, and then started speaking what I knew of the language. Typically, I mainly knew all the swear words, so he and I were commenting on all of the swear words that we both knew. We ended up in tears of hilarity over the swear words that I did know. He couldn't stop laughing at what I was saying, so I obviously got the accent right. He then told me he was going to tell his wife how I was able to distract him by telling him all the Greek swear words that the Greeks knew and used regularly.

The Iranian woman

In a recent centre, an Iranian woman and her mother came in for a blood test. The mother needed the blood test but couldn't speak much English so the daughter was there to translate. I knew only one word in Farsi, and wasn't very good at saying it because whenever I said it they would look at me with a blank look on their face.

I did the blood test and the mother knew exactly what to do. I only needed the daughter to help out with the technical aspects of some of the blood tests. As they had to wait a while due to administrative issues with the previous patient, they weren't happy in relation to the wait but thankful that the blood test was over and they could go on their day.

The Colombian woman

In a recent centre, a Colombian woman came into the centre looking to have her blood tests done. She was newly pregnant, so was getting the typical blood tests done for pregnancy. I had just finished watching a TV show about Pablo Escobar, so I was very interested to know how she felt about living in Colombia with a recent history of knowing about what Pablo Escobar had done to Colombia.

She was very obliging. She told me while I was doing the blood test on her how the situation felt for her. Colombia is now different from Pablo Escobar's time, and there have been many changes to the way drug cartels are treated.

She also told me that Colombia is no longer her home. Her roots are now in Australia, and she intended to keep it that way. She had visited to see family members, but to her it was a place to visit rather than stay.

The Filipino couple

Filipino people are different to any other culture when it comes to doing their blood tests. When a child or teenager has their blood test done, their skin is hard and smooth. Obviously, children and teenagers have no wrinkles and their skin hasn't aged, like for most people when they get older.

The skin of Filipino people is as hard as a teenager's skin, right up until way into their 50s. I'm not sure what they do, but every Filipino patient I have met has this type of skin. It's like they found the elixir of life! They don't even have any wrinkles. Few people in the community would know the exact age of a Filipino person.

In a recent centre, a Filipino couple came in for their regular blood tests. In this centre, there was a very experienced phlebotomist for a while who was Filipina. Patients still talk about her, even though she has gone in another direction in life. They all loved her. This Filipino couple was no different.

The man was relatively easy to find a vein. Even though the skin was quite hard, his vein was found with a little extra tightening of the tourniquet. I did his blood test first, and then completed all of his paperwork.

As everyone's arm is different when it comes to blood tests, many people require different skills to find a vein and then do the blood test. Some people require less skill, like the Filipino man. Other people require more skill, like his wife.

His Filipina wife has extremely difficult veins and knew it. I took one look, and decided the only way to obtain any kind of specimen was to use a blue butterfly needle. I went and got the needle and used my skill, and was thankfully successful the first time.

It was then that they compared me to the Filipina phlebotomist. They told me that I was just like her in doing blood tests. I found that to be an incredible compliment.

The Ukrainian woman

When it comes to this story, I was quite experienced but the centre was at no stage busy. I was quite used to very busy centres and had actually become quite bored. The centre was in a medical centre, and only a few doctors worked in the centre at the time so I had a lot of time on my hands. I'm the sort of person who likes to keep busy.

A woman came in for a blood test. She was originally from a different country and had an accent, so I asked her where her family was from. She told me she was born and grew up in the Ukraine. We talked about the war with Russia, and she was quite heartbroken about what was going on in the Ukraine.

As I am a humanitarian, I believe in human rights for everyone. I do not believe in war, and I do not believe in genocide. I believe all people have a right to live in peace.

This lovely woman was heartbroken at what was going on in her home country. She knew she couldn't go back to the Ukraine while Russia was bombing it, as it was too dangerous for her. She had heard nothing from anyone within the community about the war, and didn't know how anyone felt about what was going on in that part of Europe. I guess for many people Europe is very far away physically.

So I told her 'Slava Ukraini' to show her that people do know what's going on. I also showed her that others within Australia are also for human rights. I showed her Facebook posts from friends who are against war at every moment in life, and how we are all sharing around how we feel about war.

To say she was relieved was an understatement. It actually made her cry to know people think about human rights every moment of every day.

The Indian couple

There are many people from Indian descent in Australia. They bring great food, and they know how to work hard and contribute in so many different ways. When I first moved into my own place many years ago, the first food delivery I got was Indian food.

They don't just contribute with wonderful food. They are the backbone for many companies across the entirety of Australia. They also need blood tests, so I see quite a few regulars who have Indian heritage.

A couple came into the centre desperate for their first child, so they came in for many blood tests. They always came in with a smile. The woman loved seeing me because she said I put her at ease. She used to be very nervous about blood tests, but she started to get used to them.

When I first saw her, I started talking about Pixie my cat. Each time she came back for yet another blood test, she asked about Pixie. She had a massive smile on her face when she asked because she knew that talking about Pixie was a great distraction for the blood test.

I asked them how they are going. Unfortunately, they didn't have news about having a baby yet, but I hoped they would be successful soon. They deserve all the good things in life.

The Italian woman

I was at a centre with other coworkers while working as a relief. An Italian woman came into the centre looking to have her blood test done.

Duolingo had for a while worked wonders for me. There were so many languages, and I went overboard with languages for quite some time. Italian was one of those languages that I had great interest in. Even now, I get a little confused with speaking the few Spanish words I know compared to the few Italian words. They are similar in some ways, but not similar in others.

While I was doing the blood test, I started speaking in Italian some of the few words I knew, including numbers. She was delighted to hear that I tried, and corrected me when I was wrong. She even told family members in the waiting room how I was speaking a few words and they applauded me even though I wasn't very good at it.

With the blood test being completed, she went home with her family.

The Italian man

When I had first started out as a relief, I was sent to a centre that had a very large Italian population. An Italian man walked into the centre needing to have his blood test done. He had lived in Australia for many years but still couldn't shake the slight accent. Sometimes that happens with people who were born in other countries. For me, I love it.

The one thing I talk about with people from other countries is food. I love Italian food. I have been to Italy, so one story I have told Italian patients has been about the pizza over in Florence. Food is a great connector in any language.

I also told him the food that I grew up with. My mother couldn't cook for the life of her. I grew up with meat and 3 vegetables. The meat was grossly overcooked (burnt on the inside), the mashed potatoes were lumpy, and the other vegetables were cooked for 5 minutes in the microwave which meant they ended up being rubbery. It made me love hospital and plane food when I was growing up. When I moved out of my family's home, I decided long ago to try the food from other cultures with the knowledge that anything would be better than my family's cooking. I was actually quite traumatised from the cooking during my childhood. So… I talk about food from other cultures regularly.

He was very happy to talk about Italy and food. He was also very happy to talk about the Italian coffee in one of the very renowned Italian restaurants near the area. The blood test went perfectly fine, but the memory of talking about Italian food will stay with me for a long time.

Chapter 24 - Racism

There is quite a lot of racism in Australia. It's no use hiding from it, denying it, or ignoring it. Racism exists. It may be due to ignorance or jealousy. I don't quite understand the reasoning behind the racism, as I have a half Maori cousin and a half Macedonian cousin who are both awesome.

Within the last several years, some family members and I have been tracing our family history. What we found surprised us, and made us all the more interested in our backgrounds. We have certain traits that are a bit different to the typical English background, so we decided to look further.

What we found was that there was an ancestor who was Native American. There is residual DNA showing in some tests but not all. There was talk within the family about a Native American ancestor as well. So, I went digging for who it could have been.

I can only made a calculated guess on who it was and their history of how they turned up in England in the early 1700s. My guess is that one of the leaders of the East India Company kidnapped my ancestor as a child and enslaved her. She was brought back to England to become a servant, and then was raped until her daughter was born. She then disappeared from our history.

Her daughter was brought up in a church, but wasn't born there. She had a name and a knowledge of her Native American mother, but that was about it. She never knew who her mother's original family was, or where in America they came from. I am taking a very wild guess that my ancestor was Cherokee, but it's a guess and I may be wrong. At the time, the British were kidnapping and enslaving many, even with treaties. They broke every treaty they signed.

More often than not, checking out ancestors should reduce the impact of racism but we can tell that it sometimes doesn't. I am a great believer in speaking out against racism, and have done so many times.

The woman needing a blood test

I was in a day room, and had experience at the time with many patients. A woman walked into the room needing a blood test. She claimed that she was difficult to find, but I was able to find her vein quite easily. She was very happy to have found a phlebotomist who could obtain a specimen from her. She even told me at the time that she was going to come back to me for all her blood tests from then on.

As I was still going through my family ancestry, I made conversation with the patient as I usually do to distract them. I started talking about what happened to the Native Americans during the 1600s and 1700s and how horrible it was. I told her 'white people have a lot to answer for'.

She told me 'but you are white!'. She looked chagrined and surprised that a phlebotomist who could be successful with her was saying things about the European race like that. I told her 'I'm not as white as you think'.

I then told her about my family history, and how I have a little Native American ancestry. I told her how proud I was of that history, even though it was quite minimal with only a few drops of Native American blood.

I never saw her again. I'm guessing she didn't like someone telling the truth about our own race. It was probably a bit too confronting for her.

The man who pushed to the front

It was an extremely busy centre, and a really busy Saturday morning. I believe that was the day that I had been successful with more than 30 patients in the morning. I was exhausted by the end of it, that much I remember. Apart from this one experience, everything else was a blur and I wasn't sure how I survived it at the time. I definitely deserved chocolate.

The first patient I saw with a smile was a Chinese woman. She was shorter than me, and very thin. She took the first number.

All of a sudden, a very large man came up and said he was first. He said he was waiting much longer than her and he deserved to have his blood test done before her. He was really rude.

I started saying no and that he had to get in line. The woman was first and she should have gone into the room first as per my procedure. He started talking over both her and me. I was about to put my foot down and tell him to wait, when she saw the futility of arguing with such a physically large man and let him go first.

I was not happy with him or the situation. Usually, I am very friendly with patients in an effort to distract them. I remember this distinctly. I said the minimum to him at all times, even when he tried to strike up a conversation. I showed my absolute displeasure in having someone so rude in my room. He was a horrible person, and I was glad to see him go as soon as all the paperwork was properly completed. I behaved professionally because I had to, but I did the absolute bare minimum to make him comfortable. I hoped he felt every cell in my body block his every effort to try to be friendly to me.

The next patient was the lovely Chinese woman. She told me how unhappy she was with the experience. I told her I was unhappy as well, and I hadn't bothered to even talk to him while he was in the room. She then told me that she had been waiting in her car for around half an hour before the centre opened and she saw him pull up in his car at the time. She was definitely the first patient there, and he had decided that because she was Chinese, he took precedence over her.

I told her to make a complaint to my company about the situation and how offended she was. I told her she shouldn't have had to put up with such a rude and obnoxious person who was obviously guided by racism. I actually begged her to make a complaint so that my company could deal with his rude behaviour.

To conclude

It's amazing that I have been able to remember so many stories about the people who have crossed my path in the hope of finding out how their health was. From everyone looking at their general health, to real problems that are within the cog of the health system, many people from all walks of life come into the centres looking for answers.

I am not alone. There are many phlebotomists out there doing their best to help as health workers. From small babies to the elderly nearly about to pass away, patients all have one thing in common. They come to us to have their blood test.

We are the frontline workers who do our best. Sometimes we miss a vein, or we unwittingly cause pain. We cannot see underneath the veins so we try hard with our skill. Sometimes, we even hit a nerve. Everyone who takes blood has unfortunately done that at least once in their lifetime.

Sometimes, we cause bruises. We don't mean to. It just happens.

Sometimes, we are abused by patients who have waited for us. We can't help but follow our procedures to ensure that doctors get the results for each patient. Other times, we are abused because we are there and the patient is grumpy or has their own problems.

As people from all walks of life come into a collection centre looking to figure out what has been going on, my wish is for people to understand others within the community. Everyone has a story to tell, and these are a few stories of the people within the community who have experienced a blood test.

As the saying goes - be kind, because you don't know what any other person is going through.

phlebotomists to explain what the lab needs, not the doctor.

These stories are also a way for people within the community to understand some requirements in relation to having a blood test, as well as some of the procedures that we need to do to ensure accurate results are sent to their doctors. It shows that nobody is alone with the way they feel about blood tests. Most people are nervous, and that is quite ok.

Most people are terrified of blood tests. They go out of their way to procrastinate until the very last moment. Many are contacted by their doctor to ask why the blood test hadn't been done yet. Their nervousness while waiting for the "vampire" phlebotomist expands every minute they then sit in the waiting room.

As an experienced phlebotomist, over time one can accumulate many stories of interactions while someone is getting their blood test done. From the extremely nervous to the cool, calm and collected, these stories will always protect privacy. This job demands privacy of patients at all times.

Many of the stories are hilarious. Some are really sad. All show a level of humanity rarely seen outside the health industry.

To me, being a phlebotomist means that I am enacting human rights on a one on one basis. I believe in humanity, and this is one of many ways to show it. Helping a patient and their doctor by finding out what's going on is a very high level of human rights, and it gives me satisfaction to know that I am helping people.

Quite a few times, when I give reasons for procedures the patient would ask 'why didn't the doctor tell me all of this?'. The biggest reason why is because every laboratory (lab) across the country has around 5000 tests that a doctor can give to a patient to find out what's going on with them. Doctors are human, and for them to remember everything else on top of knowing every single procedure for a blood test would be impossible. It is up to

www.ingramcontent.com/pod-product-compliance
Lightning Source LLC
Chambersburg PA
CBHW040221040426
42333CB00049B/3063